THE TRANSCONTINENTAL RAILROAD IN AMERICAN HISTORY

R. Conrad Stein

Enslow Publishers, Inc.

44 Fadem Road   PO Box 38
Box 699   Aldershot
Springfield, NJ 07081 Hants GU12 6BP
USA   UK

Library of Congress Cataloging-in-Publication Data

Stein, R. Conrad.
    The Transcontinental Railroad in American history / Richard C. Stein.
       p. cm. — (In American history)
    Includes bibliographical references (p.) and index.
    Summary: Describes the building of the first railroad to join the eastern
and western part of the United States and the effect of this
transcontinental link on the future development of the country.
    ISBN 0-89490-882-0
    1. Pacific railroads—Juvenile literature. [1. Pacific railroads.
2. Railroads—History.] I. Title. II. Series.
TF25.P23S74 1997
385'.0979—dc21
                                        96-45525
                                            CIP
                                            AC

Printed in the United States of America

10 9 8 7 6 5 4 3 2 1

Illustration Credits: Christine Horning, p. 25, 112. Library of
Congress, pp. 16, 32, 34, 36, 39, 42, 73, 99, 101, 104, 109; National
Archives, pp. 6, 12, 24, 27, 62, 67, 75, 87, 93; Stanford University
Library, pp. 18, 44, 48, 51, 54, 57, 80, 82, 119; Stanford University
Museum of Art AAA, Gift of David Hewes, p. 8.

Cover Illustrations: Stanford University Library; National Archives;
Library of Congress.

★ CONTENTS ★

THE GOLDEN SPIKE

On a dusty plain just north of Salt Lake City, Utah, a crowd of well-dressed men and women mingled with workers in overalls. The dignitaries guzzled down glasses of champagne. A brass band was poised to play. Two companies of United States soldiers stood at attention. For the occasion, the plain was called Promontory Point. The date was May 10, 1869.

Promontory Point was the linkup spot where two huge railroad construction crews came together. One crew had started in California, blasted through the Sierra Nevada, bridged rivers, and carved out forests in order to build tracks to Promontory. The other crew began hammering down track in Nebraska, fought American Indians, crossed mountains, and toiled over waterless wastes to reach the meeting point. In all, some twenty thousand workers had laid 1,175 miles of track, most of it in the last three years. Now, at last, the job was over. A single line of track had been built over the western half of the United States. That line connected with existing railroad networks east of the

Dignitaries gather at Promontory Point to celebrate the "Meeting of the Rails," on May 10, 1869.

Mississippi River. It was now possible for an American to make the incredible journey between the Atlantic on the East Coast and the Pacific on the West Coast by train.

Millions of spikes had been driven into thousands of crossties to build this first transcontinental railroad. The last spike to be placed in a crosstie would be a golden one. That was the reason why the band had come to play and company officials had gathered to make speeches. Around the country people waited, breathless, to hear the news that the great railway had finally brought East and West together. The transcontinental line was a dream that had been nurtured for more than a quarter of a century. The golden spike would turn the dream into a reality. In Sacramento, California, citizens had decorated thirty locomotive engines with red, white, and blue paper. When news of the last spike came by telegraph, the train engineers were ordered to blow their whistles in unison, thereby creating a symphony of steam. In New York, one hundred cannoneers waited to fire a booming salute. In Chicago, people formed a parade that would eventually be seven miles long. At 12:27 P.M., a Promontory Point telegrapher clicked out the message: "ALMOST READY. HATS OFF. PRAYER IS BEING OFFERED."[1]

While prayers and speeches were delivered two train engines sat on the single track, facing each other.

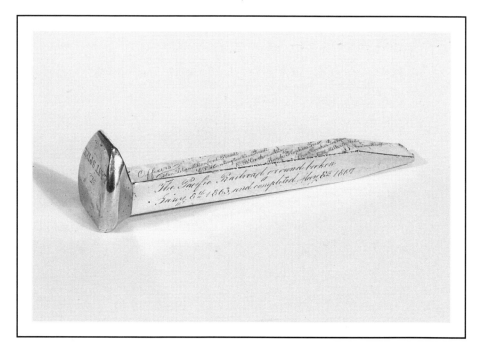

One of the engraved Golden Spikes used in the "Meeting of the Rails" ceremony.

An engine named the *Jupiter* had come from California, and another engine simply called *No. 119* had come from the East. At the end of the ritual they were slated to inch forward until their wedge-shaped pilots or cowcatchers, which protruded from the front ends, touched. Such would be the symbolic marriage of East with West, the final kissing of the bride. In faraway San Francisco, the writer Bret Harte pictured the two engines hissing on their tracks, and began a poem:

> *What was it the Engines said,*
> *Pilots touching,—head to head*
> *Facing on a single track,*
> *Half a world behind each back?*[2]

2

SEA TO SHINING SEA

I want you to write me a great deal about our little girl. I often think of her when night has hushed all sounds. . . . Poor child! I shall never forget [her] expression . . . when I took her in my arms and kissed her on the morning I left home.[1]

—From a letter written in 1850 by a California gold miner named William Swain to his wife in Niagara Falls, New York

Manifest Destiny

In the 1840s, the excitement of western expansion gripped the country. "Our population is rolling toward the shores of the Pacific with an impetus greater than what we realize,"[2] said Congressman John C. Calhoun in an 1843 speech. The drive toward the Pacific came to be called America's manifest destiny. The term meant that westward expansion was the country's inevitable future, as if it were a commandment issued by God. The spirit of manifest destiny encouraged America to absorb the Oregon Territory and to persuade the fledgling independent nation of Texas to join the Union. Manifest destiny was a major cause of the war with Mexico, fought from 1846 to 1848. At the conclusion of that war, America acquired the southwestern states and California. With California in its fold, the country now spanned the continent. But the promise of manifest destiny would be unfulfilled until Americans settled the vast and relatively empty lands of the West.

When the United States took possession of California, Los Angeles was a sleepy village and San Francisco a tiny port. Then, in January 1848, a ranch foreman discovered a piece of shining metal on Johann Sutter's property near Sacramento. The speck of metal was only the size of a pea, but it was pure gold. News of the find quickly reached the eastern states and spread to other countries, too. Hunger for gold triggered a human stampede. In 1849 alone, some eighty-five thousand adventurers swarmed to California seeking their fortune. Those who arrived in 1849 were called the 49ers. The vast majority of 49ers found no gold at all. But they were the spearhead of manifest destiny, and they wrote a colorful chapter in American history. As they started out on their journey, many of the gold seekers sang a song to the tune of *O! Susannah!*

> *O! Californy!*
> *That's the land for me!*
> *I'm bound for Sacramento*
> *With my washbowl on my knee.*[3]

Miners like these at a Nevada mining camp often suffered from homesickness and feelings of isolation, as they were separated from their families for months or years on end.

A prospector from the East took one of three possible routes to get to the Promised Land of California: one, walking the length of the country; two, sailing on ships going around Cape Horn at the tip of South America; or three, sailing to Panama, crossing overland to the Pacific, and then catching a ship heading north to San Francisco. All three routes were filled with perils, and they took at least six months of travel time. Despite the hardships, prospectors kept coming, filled with dreams and hope.

Between 1847 and 1850 the population of California swelled from 15,000 to 92,497 people. California became a state in 1850. Ten years later its population had reached 379,994.

Almost all of the California pioneers suffered from homesickness and a depressing feeling of isolation. They had families in places like Pennsylvania, New Jersey, and Ohio. Letters from those eastern states took eight months or more to reach California gold camps. Babies were born, people died, relatives of the miners got married long before the Californians received word of these important events. Returning to one's home state for a visit meant a very expensive and time-consuming journey.

Promise of the Railroads

Certainly a railroad to the East would cure California's isolation. But building such a railroad over the western deserts and mountains seemed to be a nearly impossible task. As early as 1838, a railroad surveyor named John Plumbe suggested laying tracks from the East right up to the Pacific shore. A member of Congress told Plumbe that his proposal would be like "building a railroad to the moon."[4]

Well before the Gold Rush, train travel had captured the nation's imagination. At the time, the overwhelming majority of Americans lived on farms or in rural villages.

SOURCE DOCUMENT

From a letter dated August 6, 1849:

SENATOR BENTON AND OTHER BIG MEN MAY TALK AND HUMBUG THE COUNTRY AND YOU GREENHORNS ABOUT A RAILROAD TO THE PACIFIC, BUT IF YOU AND I LIVE A THOUSAND YEARS, WE WILL NEVER SEE THE RESEMBLANCE EVEN OF SUCH A THING. THERE IS NOT TIMBER ALONG THIS ROUTE TO LAY THE TRACK HALF PART OF THE WAY; AND IF THERE WAS, IT WOULD COST MORE MONEY TO BUILD IT THAN THERE IS IN THE U.S. MEN WHO COULD BUILD A RAILROAD TO THE MOON PERHAPS COULD BUILD ONE OVER THESE MOUNTAINS, BUT I DOUBT IT. YOU MAY THINK YOU HAVE SEEN MOUNTAINS AND GONE OVER THEM, BUT YOU NEVER SAW ANYTHING BUT A SMALL HILL COMPARED WITH WHAT I HAVE CROSSED OVER, AND IT IS SAID THE WORST IS YET TO COME. BUT NEVER MIND, GOLD LIES AHEAD.[5]

This letter, dated August 6, 1849, demonstrates how many of those who rushed to the gold fields of California thought the idea of building a railroad to link the East and West was an impossible dream.

Many lived out their entire lives without venturing more than fifty miles from the place where they were born. Then came the trains—the thundering and steaming Iron Horses—which rushed people to far-flung cities and states over gleaming rails. Speaking to Congress in 1846, one representative likened the train to a glorious beast from the pages of mythology:

The Iron Horse with the wings of wind, his nostrils distended with flame, vomiting fire and smoke, trembling with power . . . flies from one end of the continent to the other in less time than our ancestry required to visit a neighboring city.[6]

By 1850, American railroad companies had built more than nine thousand miles of track. This entire network was constructed in the eastern states. But the trend of the railroad companies followed the spirit of manifest destiny and pushed ever westward. In 1854, a railroad line reached the banks of the Mississippi River at Rock Island, Illinois. A railway linking the Atlantic and the Mississippi seemed miraculous in 1854. Many Americans alive at the time could remember when George Washington was president, and no steam locomotive ran anywhere in the world. Given this fantastic progress, was it not possible to build tracks all the way to California?

Theodore Judah—Keeper of the Dream

During the 1820s, in Troy, New York, a young boy often sat on a church step deep in thought. The boy was named Theodore Judah. His father, an Episcopal minister, always told his son that a life without a goal is a life without meaning. In his youth, Theodore chose a practical profession. He decided to be an engineer. But he never forgot his father's zeal concerning the need for a mission in life. He would not be satisfied until his work as an engineer produced something monumental,

Where no railroad existed, cargo was hauled in barges rowed by muscular men.

something that would serve as a grand testament that his life had fulfilled a purpose.

Just a few blocks from the church, another young boy sold newspapers on a street corner. His name was Charles Crocker. Muscular and loud even as a youngster, Crocker attracted newspaper buyers by shouting the headlines in a booming voice. Did Crocker and Judah know each other? Probably not, even though they were close to the same age. They lived in different worlds. Crocker was a slum dweller and a street fighter. He had only a few years of schooling. Judah, on the other hand, had a good education and enjoyed the niceties of life.

As a young engineer, Judah became a surveyor for a company that was building a railroad between the cities of Troy and Schenectady in New York. On the job he learned the principles of grading—leveling land before track could be laid down. Rails required a hard, flat surface to withstand the weight of a fully loaded train. Without a proper surface the rails would simply sink into the ground after a few years of use. Also, locomotives of the time lacked the power to pull cars uphill, which forced railroad builders to construct tracks around hills or to dig canyons (cuts) through them. In addition to grading, Judah mastered the mechanics of bridge-building. Most important, he developed a keen eye for terrain, and could quickly determine the best route to construct a section of track.

In 1854, Judah and his wife, Anna, sailed to California. There Judah helped to build the state's first railroad, a line that ran about fifty-two miles from Sacramento to the town of Marysville. Although it was tiny, the railroad filled Judah with hope. Even before coming to California, he had nurtured a dream that he would someday build a railroad across the vast lands of the West, thereby uniting the country. Only this mammoth task would satisfy his sense of destiny. His

The possibility of travel on speeding trains excited the American imagination.

wife, Anna, later said, "He had always talked, read, and studied the problem of the railway to the Pacific. He would say, 'It is going to be built and I'm going to have something to do with it.' "[7]

Judah scouted the land east of Sacramento, California, looking for a route to build the railway of his dreams. He encountered the rugged Sierra Nevada mountain range, which stood like a jagged wall, barring passage to the East. Even he—perhaps the best railroad surveyor in the country—could find no easy path through these miles of craggy cliffs. Yet he insisted that construction must begin. In Sacramento, Judah approached bankers and other financiers, asking for money to start the railroad-building project. The bankers dismissed his idea as a wild fantasy. In fact, many of them were offended by the passion Judah displayed when discussing his favorite subject. The young engineer sounded like a preacher equating the railroad with a golden path leading toward heaven. Powerful Californians started calling him "Crazy Judah."

Probably, Judah never asked his one-time neighbor Charles Crocker for financial help. In 1850, Crocker was one of those fearless individuals who walked westward when news of the Gold Rush broke. Instead of dashing out to the goldfields, Crocker opened a hardware store in Sacramento. He specialized in supplying miners with tools for digging gold. His store thrived. Always a gambler, Crocker looked for ways to invest his surplus money. Surely he would have listened to Judah's plans, but there is no record that the two ever met before 1860. Yet the day would come when Crocker, the bullheaded businessman, and Judah the dreamer would unite to build a great railroad.

*S*wiftly we sped along the iron track— Rock Island appeared in sight—the whistle sounded. . . . The cars moved on—the bridge was reached—"We're on the bridge—see the mighty Mississippi rolling on beneath"— and all eyes were fastened on the mighty parapets of the magnificent bridge, over which we glided in solemn silence.[1]

THE PACIFIC RAILROAD ACT

—A reporter from the *Rock Island Advertiser* who, in 1856, rode on the first passenger train to cross the Mississippi River

War!

By the late 1850s, more and more Americans were convinced that a railroad to the Pacific would someday be built. Congress had already authorized several surveys to determine a route for tracks running westward from the Mississippi River. Many members of Congress argued that the best route lay across the flat lands of Iowa to the Missouri River at Council Bluffs. The tracks would then follow the banks of the

Platte River, and wind their way through the Rocky Mountains until they reached the Great Salt Lake. From the Salt Lake, rails would be built westward toward the Sierras. This path roughly paralleled the Oregon and California Trails, which had been used for decades by westward travelers. Centuries earlier, American Indian trading parties used the same route.

But politics complicated the decision-making process concerning the railroad's course. In the 1850s, America was not one nation, but two factions dangerously divided over the explosive issue of slavery. In the South were slave-holding states that looked to their Congress members in Washington, D.C., to pass proslavery laws. Politicians from Northern states strove to weaken or abolish the slavery system. Thus, Washington before the Civil War was a battleground between pro and antislavery forces, and the proposed transcontinental railroad added fuel to an already roaring fire.

The Southern forces in Congress insisted that the Pacific railroad cross the Mississippi at Memphis, Tennessee, and then begin its western leg through the southwestern territories. It was supposed by everyone that the railroad would attract thousands of settlers. Towns and cities would spring up alongside its tracks. New states would emerge. Southern congressmen hoped the settlers would be from the Southern states, and therefore would be proslavery. Thus the new states created by the Pacific railroad would be slave states. A railway across the Southwest instead of the Northwest was vital for Southern interests.

The debate between Southern and Northern forces raged on, stifling a decision by Congress. It seemed that politics, not the forbidding terrain, would doom the Pacific railroad. Then, finally, the fuse that had been smoldering throughout the country reached the explosive point. Two years before he became president, Abraham Lincoln declared, "A house divided against itself cannot stand. I believe this government cannot endure, permanently, half slave and half free."[2] History proved his statement to be all too accurate. Lincoln was elected president in 1860. On the day he took his oath of office seven Southern states had already seceded from the Union. A month later, Fort Sumter was fired upon, and America erupted into war.

No conflict in the nation's history was more costly than was the Civil War. Over the course of four years the country was locked in a whirlwind of bloodshed as one tragic battle followed another. For the North, the terrible war proved the value of railroads. At the time the war began, the North had more than twenty-five thousand miles of track, compared to the South's ten thousand. Also, most of the factories that built locomotives and cars were located in the North.

This photograph shows how Fort Sumter looked after the bombardment that started the Civil War.

Southern soldiers fought bravely, but the North's superior railroad system kept its armies far better supplied.

War raging across the land cut off debate in Congress regarding the route of the Pacific railway. With no Southern representatives in Washington to protest, Congress decided on the Northern route. In 1862, Congress passed the Pacific Railroad Act. The act authorized two railroad companies—the Central Pacific in the West and the Union Pacific in the East— to build a transcontinental line. Many details still had

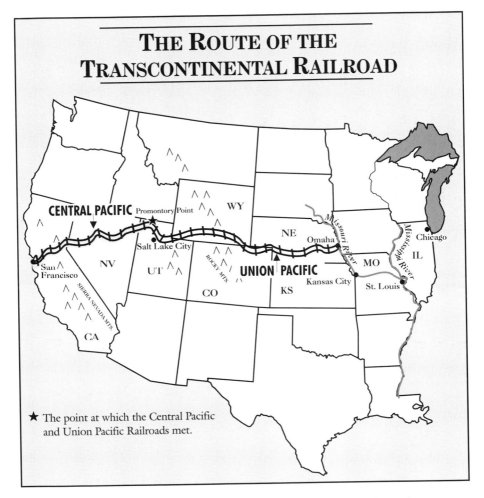

THE ROUTE OF THE TRANSCONTINENTAL RAILROAD

CENTRAL PACIFIC Promontory Point

Salt Lake City

San Francisco

NV

UT

CA

SIERRA NEVADA MTS.

ROCKY MTS.

CO

WY

NE

Omaha

Missouri River

UNION PACIFIC

Kansas City

KS

MO

St. Louis

IL

Chicago

Mississippi River

★ The point at which the Central Pacific and Union Pacific Railroads met.

The route that was finally decided upon for the transcontinental railraod crossed the plains and mountains of the United States.

to be ironed out. Of course, everyone knew that the war would delay construction. But at last Congress had determined a route and agreed to build a railroad destined to unite the nation.

Interestingly, during congressional arguments concerning the route, almost no one in Washington mentioned the American Indians living along the path the railroad would take. While there were few white settlers west of the Mississippi, the land there had been the domain of the Plains peoples for centuries. In addition, many other American Indian nations had recently been pushed across the Mississippi by white expansion. Treaties with those nations often contained poetic language giving the western lands to the American Indians for "as long as the grass shall grow and the rivers shall run."

The Central Pacific

The Civil War, in all its horror, did not touch isolated California. There, plans for the western leg of the transcontinental railroad were made almost without regard for the great conflict that was tearing the rest of the country apart. A leading figure in the early stages of the western segment was Theodore Judah. No longer called "Crazy Judah," the railroad enthusiast had persuaded four of California's richest men to invest money in the project. The four were Leland

The value of railroads became evident as the North and South tried to get supplies to their troops during the Civil War. This photograph shows a Civil War railroad yard.

Stanford, who was elected governor of California in 1861; Mark Hopkins, who had started a miners' supply store in a tent and built it into a multimillion-dollar business; Collis P. Huntington, a storekeeper and Hopkins's partner; and the self-made millionaire who had once lived in Troy, New York, Charles Crocker. These men were known as the Big Four. They dominated the building of the western portion of the railway, and they ruled the finances and politics of California for years afterward.

In 1861, the Big Four and Theodore Judah formed the Central Pacific Railroad of California. The company's long-range goal was to build eastward toward the Mississippi. Its short-range plan was to reach the newly developed silver mines in Nevada. All the members of the Big Four had made their fortunes during the great Gold Rush. Now the gold in California had been pretty well played out. The Big Four hoped that Nevada's silver would provide the next bonanza.

From the beginning it was determined that the federal government would help the two railroad companies who were building the Pacific railroad. Government leaders believed the job was too enormous to leave in private hands alone. In 1859, the army officer William Tecumseh Sherman, who later became one of the North's greatest field commanders, surveyed the Sierra Nevada range in California looking for a possible railroad passage. Like Theodore Judah before him, Sherman saw the same wall of unbroken cliffs. Sherman wrote:

> I now assert my belief that the great railroad will not receive enough net profits to pay interest on its cost . . . It is a work of giants, and Uncle Sam is the only giant I know who can or should grapple with the subject.[3]

The Pacific Railroad Act granted the Central Pacific and the Union Pacific generous amounts of free land and money in the form of loans and subsidies. The money was to be given on a sliding scale: $16,000 for every mile of track the company laid over flat land, $32,000 per mile over hill country, and $48,000 per mile in the mountains. This sliding scale would seem to benefit the Central Pacific, because it had to build in rugged mountain terrain.

Never before in the nation's history had the government provided such massive assistance to a privately financed construction project. Many Americans worried that this close cooperation between government and railroad financiers would lead to corruption. At the very beginning of the venture, their fears were confirmed when the Central Pacific submitted a doctored map to Washington. Company mapmakers conveniently moved the Sierra mountains

Excerpt from the Pacific Railway Act, July 1, 1862:

BE IT ENACTED, THAT . . . "THE UNION PACIFIC RAILROAD COMPANY" . . . IS HEREBY AUTHORIZED AND EMPOWERED TO LAY OUT, CONSTRUCT, FURNISH, MAINTAIN AND ENJOY A CONTINUOUS RAILROAD AND TELEGRAPH . . . UPON THE ROUTE AND TERMS HEREINAFTER PROVIDED. . . .

SEC. 9. THAT THE LEAVENWORTH, PAWNEE AND WESTERN RAILROAD COMPANY OF KANSAS ARE HEREBY AUTHORIZED TO CONSTRUCT A RAILROAD AND TELEGRAPH LINE . . . UPON THE SAME TERMS AND CONDITIONS IN ALL RESPECTS AS ARE PROVIDED [FOR CONSTRUCTION OF THE UNION PACIFIC RAILROAD]. . . . THE CENTRAL PACIFIC RAILROAD COMPANY OF CALIFORNIA ARE HEREBY AUTHORIZED TO CONSTRUCT A RAILROAD AND TELEGRAPH LINE FROM THE PACIFIC COAST . . . TO THE EASTERN BOUNDARIES OF CALIFORNIA, UPON THE SAME TERMS AND CONDITIONS IN ALL RESPECTS [AS ARE PROVIDED FOR THE UNION PACIFIC RAILROAD].

SEC. 11. THAT FOR THREE HUNDRED MILES OF SAID ROAD MOST MOUNTAINOUS AND DIFFICULT OF CONSTRUCTION, TO WIT: ONE HUNDRED AND FIFTY MILES WESTERLY FROM THE EASTERN BASE OF THE ROCKY MOUNTAINS, AND ONE HUNDRED AND FIFTY MILES EASTWARDLY FROM THE WESTERN BASE OF THE SIERRA NEVADA MOUNTAINS . . . THE BONDS TO BE ISSUED TO AID IN THE CONSTRUCTION THEREOF SHALL BE TREBLE THE NUMBER PER MILE HEREINBEFORE PROVIDED . . . ; AND BETWEEN THE SECTIONS LAST NAMED OF ONE HUNDRED AND FIFTY MILES EACH, THE CONSTRUCTION THEREOF SHALL BE DOUBLE THE NUMBER PER MILE FIRST MENTIONED. . . .[4]

In 1862, the United States decided to support a plan to build a transcontinental railroad, linking East and West. This is an excerpt from the 1862 Pacific Railway Act that granted the Union Pacific and the Central Pacific Railroad companies the authority to build the railroad.

about twenty-three miles east of where they actually stood. That way the company received the bonus payment for mountainous terrain—$48,000 per mile—even though it would be laying track in the Sacramento Valley, land that was as flat as a kitchen table. Theodore Judah got wind of the mountain-moving trickery, and was enraged. Judah believed that building the transcontinental railroad was his God-given mission in life. The members of the Big Four, he discovered, were motivated entirely by money.

The Union Pacific

The principal stockholder of the Union Pacific Railroad was Thomas Durant, a New York financier and an experienced builder of railroads. As a young man, Durant had studied medicine and received a degree. However, early in his career he found treating sick people to be distasteful, and became an investor instead. Still, he enjoyed being called "Doctor" Durant.

Durant was a master at manipulating politicians. He believed that the transcontinental railroad would bloom into the biggest money game in Washington. To win favors from political leaders he doled out shares in the Union Pacific Railroad. He also gave members of Congress and other insiders tips as to the exact route the railroad would take. With this information, an insider could buy up seemingly useless property at a bargain

This photograph shows early progress in the construction of the Central Pacific Line.

price, wait for the rail line to pass through and make it valuable, and then sell the land at a handsome profit.

Land, even more than money, was the greatest windfall the Union Pacific received from the government. To build their tracks, both companies were given—at first—a belt of land almost ten miles wide, absolutely free. They also had timber rights and free use of mining on the land. For the railroads, this free land was a self-financing bonanza. Farms and villages would certainly develop along the railroad line. The railroads could sell their freely given land to the settlers, and thereby pay for the cost of track construction.

In the East—the Union Pacific's territory—the land grant was a bigger gold mine than it was in the West. Settlers had already begun to push into the potential farm country beyond the Mississippi and Missouri Rivers. The thought of a rail line stretching into the western prairies triggered a flurry of land speculation by Washington insiders. All the land speculators remembered the lesson of Chicago. Railroads reached Chicago in 1854, when the city had a population of thirty thousand. Ten years later the city had zoomed to one hundred twenty-five thousand, and large property owners became millionaires. Speculators now wondered how many other potential Chicagos lay in the western lands.

The Union Pacific begins its work.

Even President Abraham Lincoln stood to profit by land he owned near present-day Omaha, Nebraska. Long before being elected president, Lincoln had received land in frontier Nebraska as settlement for a legal debt. The president's secretary of the interior, John P. Usher, recorded a conversation between Lincoln and Thomas Durant. Durant had suggested a route for the railroad that passed by Omaha. Pointing at Omaha on a map, Lincoln said, "I have got a quarter section of land right across there, and if I fix it [the railroad] there, they will say I have done it to benefit my land. But I will fix it there anyhow."[5] Lincoln had no desire to profit from the Pacific Railroad. But such was the money-making power of the project that Lincoln stood to gain funds, almost by accident.

Unlike Lincoln, Thomas Durant was in the railroad construction business strictly for the money. Before the railroad building began he formed a supply company called Crédit Mobilier of America. The major function of Crédit Mobilier was to sell goods to the Union Pacific. It sold items at inflated prices, with Durant picking up the profits. For example, Durant might buy shovels from a hardware store at five dollars each, and give them to Crédit Mobilier. Then, as chief of the Union Pacific, he would order the Union Pacific to buy the shovels from Crédit Mobilier for ten dollars each. This way Durant kept five dollars in profits—profits he did not have to share with fellow stockholders of the Union Pacific. The practice was devious, but not illegal. Crédit Mobilier was a device that Durant hoped would make him a very wealthy man.

Fortunately for the Union Pacific, not all its officers were interested only in self-enrichment. Early in the construction program, Durant hired Grenville Dodge, a construction engineer with both leadership and surveying experience, to be the railroad's chief engineer. Dodge proved to be a no-nonsense construction boss. He also had the vision to grasp what the transcontinental railroad meant for the

This is one artist's fanciful conception of the railroad line running Through to the Pacific.

country. In many respects, Dodge was the Union Pacific's idealist, as Theodore Judah was with the Central Pacific.

Both railroad companies were blessed with other men who saw nobility in the building effort. The transcontinental line needed dedicated people because, as General Sherman said, building it would require the "work of giants."

The Central Pacific Railroad Company advertises for 5000 laborers to work upon the road . . . It is the intention of the company to employ at once as many men as can be advantageously worked.[1]

—A "help wanted" ad placed in a California newspaper in January 1865

THE CENTRAL PACIFIC MAKES TRACKS

East from Sacramento

A heavy rain turned the streets of Sacramento into rivers of mud on the morning of January 8, 1863. But by noon a bright sun was blazing. Crews scattered hay around a speakers' platform so that well-dressed spectators would not dirty their clothes in the muck. A gala groundbreaking ceremony was to be held this day, as the official start of the Central Pacific's effort to build its portion of the transcontinental railroad. Just days earlier on January 1, the Emancipation Proclamation—which freed slaves in territories still at war with the Union—took effect. Four weeks before that, Northern forces were severely beaten in a battle against the Southern armies at Fredericksburg, Virginia. Despite these monumental events, officials were determined that nothing would overshadow the party thrown by the Central Pacific Railroad in California.

Governor Leland Stanford, elegant in his top hat, gave a speech: "The day is not far distant when the Pacific will be bound to the Atlantic by iron bands that shall consolidate and strengthen the ties of nationality and advance with giant strides the prosperity of our country."[2] Charles Crocker also spoke. This was long before the development of loudspeakers, but Crocker could be heard half a mile away even without amplification. Other lesser officials took their turns on the speakers' stand. Significantly, in isolated California, almost no one in the parade of speakers mentioned the Civil War that was raging in the East.

In many ways the official groundbreaking was a hollow event, because the Central Pacific was woefully unprepared to begin construction. Two major problems haunted the company: first, it lacked material; second, it lacked a labor force. In California, there were no factories that built train engines, rails, or even the spikes to drive a rail into a crosstie. All these materials had to be shipped in sailing vessels from port cities in the eastern states. In the East, railroad

This is a view of the single-track Central Pacific line as it passed through Pino, California.

equipment was in short supply because all such goods were being consumed by the war effort. Labor was even a more crucial problem for the Central Pacific. Men had come to California with dreams of striking it rich in the goldfields. Few Californians were interested in working on a railroad line. Because of these shortages, rails were not laid out of Sacramento until October 1863, ten months after the groundbreaking ceremony.

When work finally began, each member of the Big Four assumed a role. Leland Stanford was president of the Central Pacific. Because of his other job—governor of California—Stanford was able to secure favors from the state. Collis P. Huntington was vice president of the company. He spent most of the construction years in Washington, D.C., where he lobbied for more government funds, and in New York City, where he bought equipment for the Central Pacific. Huntington was able to communicate with company headquarters over the transcontinental telegraph line, which was completed in 1861. Mark Hopkins was the company's treasurer. During the Gold Rush, he had made millions selling shovels and pans to miners. Now he kept careful accounts of every keg of nails used by company crews. Charles Crocker served as construction boss. Although he had no training in railroad building, he knew how to handle men. Crocker weighed two hundred fifty pounds, was built like a bulldog, and could outshout a foghorn. When his temper was roused he settled arguments with his fists, a trait that brought Crocker respect among the raw pioneers of California.

Missing from the Central Pacific's list of officers was Theodore Judah. From the beginning Judah looked upon building the railroad the way a great artist contemplated creating a painting. To him the task ahead was an inspiration, not a mere job. Angered by the money-grubbing attitudes of the Big Four, Judah sold his shares in the Central Pacific to Charles Crocker. He then set out for New York City, where he hoped to borrow enough money to buy out the Big Four and build a railroad better fitted to his dreams. Judah chose the Panama route to reach the East Coast. While crossing the jungle in Panama he was bitten by a mosquito bearing the yellow fever virus. Theodore Judah died in New York City on November 2, 1863. Ironically, Judah—the man obsessed by a dream—lost his life because the nation did not yet have a transcontinental railroad which could have carried him to the East in safety.

From a Great Wall to a Great Railroad

Day by day the Central Pacific's tracks inched out of Sacramento. Railroad building in those days required

Here, Central Pacific workers have dug a minor cut some sixty miles from Sacramento.

huge crews, and the work pace was intense. The path the tracks took first had to be graded. Grading meant the path was made smooth, hard, and as level as possible. This required hundreds of men pounding the earth with shovels and crushing rocks with hammers and picks. Trains were unable to climb steep inclines. Therefore "cuts"—man-made canyons—had to be dug through hills. Invariably there were rivers, gorges, and dry creeks to cross. This meant bridges must be erected. Early in the project the Central Pacific's crews built a long and complex bridge over the American River near Sacramento, and the men dug the awesome Bloomer Cut through a hill near the town of Newcastle, California. The Bloomer Cut was a wedge-shaped slice in the earth that measured 800 feet long and 63 feet deep. Crocker's crews had to blast the ground loose with explosives, dig it out, and haul it away in wheelbarrows or in dump carts pulled by mules. Given the difficult terrain they had to conquer, the Central Pacific's workers had done well. But in early 1865—more than two years after the groundbreaking—the company's tracks stretched only forty miles out of Sacramento.

Although they desperately needed workers, the owners of the Central Pacific clung to a policy of hiring white men only. At the time, it was generally believed that only white men had the discipline as well as the

This photograph shows the awesome Bloomer Cut, which was the first great man-made canyon created by Central Pacific crews.

brawn to complete large construction projects. The company followed this policy despite the fact that white Americans demanded high wages and were quick to strike if they thought they were treated unfairly. Worse yet, the whites had come to California as prospectors, and were still filled with Gold Rush dreams. When news spread that the silver fields in Nevada were even richer than expected, the whites simply left their work gangs and headed for the newest Promised Land. Out of dire need, Charles Crocker got the notion to hire Chinese workers. He explained his idea to his top foreman, a professional railroad builder from Vermont by the name of James Strobridge. At first the foreman dismissed Crocker's suggestion. He argued that the Chinese were too frail to perform the rugged physical work demanded by railroad building. Crocker reminded him that at one time they built the biggest wall on earth: the Great Wall of China. Crocker later wrote:

> It was four or five months . . . before I could get Mr. Strobridge to take Chinamen. Finally he took in fifty Chinamen, and a while after that he took in fifty more. Then they did so well . . . that he got more and more.[3]

James Strobridge soon came to believe that the Chinese were among the best workers in the world.

At the time of the Civil War, some forty-five thousand men and women of Chinese descent lived in

SOURCE DOCUMENT

From a letter dated July 19, 1850:

THERE ARE THOSE TO WHOM MINING HAS ALL THE EXCITEMENT OF GAMBLING, AND WHO, AS THEY WOULD BUY A LOTTERY TICKET IN THE HOPE OF DRAWING THE HIGHEST PRIZE, SO NOW PERSEVERE, IN SPITE OF ILL LUCK AND THE WARNING OF OTHERS, FULLY EXPECTING THE ADVENT OF THE DAY WHEN THEY, AND THEY ALONE, SHALL BE REWARDED WITH AMPLE SOIL. THERE ARE THOUSANDS WHO AT HOME WOULD BE OBLIGED TO WORK FOR A DOLLAR A DAY AND BE UNDER THE EYE OF THE OVERSEER, AND WHO, CONSEQUENTLY, ARE NOT DISAPPOINTED AT BEING THEIR OWN MASTERS.[4]

In this letter, one miner illustrates why it was so difficult to persuade white workers to leave the gold mines for jobs as laborers on the railroad.

northern California. The majority had arrived during the Gold Rush days. They earned a meager living by finding tiny amounts of gold dust in the dug-up earth that white miners had left behind after sifting through it in search of gold chunks. When the gold finally played out, the Chinese took menial jobs as house servants and farmworkers. California had never permitted slavery, but in effect Chinese workers took the place of slaves. A newspaper called *The Sacramento Union* claimed the average Chinese laborer earned between four and eight dollars a month, a scale far lower than that for whites. Furthermore, white Californians refused to live as neighbors with the Chinese, which forced them to reside in shacks built out of discarded crates and scrap wood.

Trouble brewed when the first Chinese reported to work on the Central Pacific. White workers, especially the Irish, hurled insults at the newcomers. In the eastern states, the Irish immigrants had long been the underdogs, the disadvantaged and unskilled workers who were forced to take back-breaking jobs for low pay. It was only in California that they could enjoy what they thought to be the proper rights and privileges of white men. The Chinese workers, most of whom wore light-blue cotton clothing and dishpan-shaped hats, smiled and said nothing while the whites barraged them with catcalls. It was a blessing that only a handful of them spoke English. Strobridge and Crocker decided to work the Chinese in separate gangs from the whites. They feared that a riot would break out if the two races toiled side by side.

The average Chinese laborer at the time stood about five feet tall, and weighed perhaps one hundred twenty pounds. Central Pacific foremen shook their heads in doubt, wondering how these tiny men would ever be able to build a railroad. But the Chinese worked steadily, not pausing even to wipe the sweat off their foreheads. Two or three times a day a group of

This Chinese worker is a member of a Central Pacific tunnel-digging gang.

young boys would arrive carrying two buckets tied to the ends of a stick. The buckets contained lukewarm tea. (White workers relieved their thirst with water, which was often a source of illness.) Crew members stopped for a moment, sipped cups of tea, and then returned immediately to work. At the end of a week the Chinese graders had prepared a longer path for tracks than had a nearby white crew. Whites considered it insulting to be outworked by the little men from Asia, and they increased their pace. A lively competition developed between the races. Crocker and Strobridge smiled at the results.

At night, the Chinese camped in separate compounds from the whites. Most whites found their living habits to be baffling. They employed their own cooks to make pots of rice and side dishes of salted cabbage. Their food alone was curious to the whites who were accustomed to boiled beef, beans, and potatoes. But the ritual they observed prior to eating seemed even more preposterous. Before they ate, each Chinese worker stripped naked and bathed in barrels of water provided by the cooks. Camp rules were clear, even to the onlookers. Every man must be thoroughly washed and dressed in clean clothes before the cooks would allow him to eat. The white workers, who took only a few baths in the course of a year, laughed at this insistence on cleanliness.

The Central Pacific paid its Chinese workers about thirty dollars a month, which was five dollars less than the average white received. But the Chinese demanded and got some special considerations. Where the whites were paid in American dollar bills, the Chinese received their wages in gold. The Chinese also required the company to provide their food. This meant that Central Pacific clerks had to deal with Chinese merchants in San Francisco and buy large quantities of goods the clerks had never heard of before: bamboo shoots, cuttlefish, dried oysters, Chinese bacon, and dried abalone. In April 1865, Leland Stanford was able to boast:

> The greater portion of the laborers employed by us are Chinese. . . . Without them it would be impossible to complete the western portion of the [transcontinental railroad]. As a class they are quiet, peaceable, patient, industrious, and economical—ready and apt to learn all the different kinds of work required in railroad building. . . . They soon become as efficient as white laborers.[5]

As work continued, any Chinese male in California who wished to work on the railroad was hired by the Central Pacific. And the company made arrangements to import even more laborers from China.

The Challenge of the Sierras

By the summer of 1865, Central Pacific workers had constructed an advance camp at the settlement of

This photograph shows a Central Pacific track-laying crew at work.

Colfax, California, fifty-five miles east of Sacramento. Colfax lay at the base of the mighty Sierra Nevada. There was no easy way through this mountain range. Cuts had to be dug and gullies and ravines filled in. The most painstaking task of all would be tunneling through the series of towering peaks. Plans called for boring fifteen tunnels, the longest one being more than fifteen hundred feet.

Even building tracks to reach the base of the Sierras was a daunting job. No trail, not even a goat path, led to the mountains. The Sierra foothills were covered with trees—virgin pines whose trunks measured eight feet across, and redwoods that were even thicker. The raw beauty of this forest, which had stood undisturbed for hundreds of years, was awesome. But construction engineers looked upon the trees as obstacles barring the path of the railroad, not as cathedrals of nature. The great trees were cut down and hauled away. Hardwoods were sawed up to make crossties. Other trunks were used as supports for bridges. Roots of the giants had to be chopped at with axes and finally tugged out of the ground by men and teams of horses. When a path was finally cleared through the forest at Colfax, workers stood in front of a cliff which rose almost a quarter mile high. The cliff stood on the east side of the American River. With no way to circumvent it, crews had to carve a cut through the wall of rock. The white workers, many of whom had been sailors in the past, called the cliff "Cape Horn."

To create a cut in Cape Horn, workers were lowered over the cliff on ropes. There, dangling from the dizzying heights, they pounded sharpened iron rods into the cliffside with hammers. When they had drilled out a deep enough hole they "tamped" blasting powder into it, set fuses, and when done shouted, "Haul away!" Crews on the top then pulled the workers to safety, and a portion of the cliff was blasted loose. When the smoke of the explosions cleared the men were sent down the ropes again like dozens of spiders on strands of a web. It was an agonizingly slow process, one that consumed the labor of hundreds of the Central Pacific's best workers.

At Cape Horn, the Chinese once more came to the rescue of the Central Pacific. Up to this point the Chinese had been passive in controlling the course of the project. They did as they were ordered and asked no questions. While watching the white crews tackle the cliffs, however, one Chinese leader gingerly approached construction boss James Strobridge. Through an interpreter, he suggested that Chinese workers could do as well at performing these cliff-hanging tasks which the whites had nicknamed "rock work." He explained that in years past Chinese laborers had built fortresses for warlords along the

A Central Pacific train passes through the American River country where the very difficult "rock work" was performed.

crevices of China's Yangtze River. Much of the Yangtze terrain was similar to this great cliff. Working with blasting powder would pose no problem because gunpowder was a Chinese invention, and all the men had made firecrackers when they were boys. Strobridge, who was warming up to the Chinese, decided to give them a chance. He was confused, though, when the Chinese foreman asked that a shipment of reeds be brought up from San Francisco.

The Chinese camp buzzed with activity the night the reeds arrived. Working by the light of campfires, the men wove the reeds into wide baskets, each about three feet deep. These were the same kind of baskets that their ancestors had used to carry goods for more than a thousand years. Here in America the sturdy baskets would find a new purpose. In the morning, dozens of Chinese laborers climbed into their baskets and were lowered by ropes over the cliff at Cape Horn. There, standing inside the baskets, they commenced the tedious rock work. As the weeks went by, the workers decorated their baskets with Chinese symbols designed to ward off evil spirits and protect them from danger. The symbols did not always work. Now and then the sound of a scream followed by a splash pierced the river valley, and a basket and a dishpan-shaped hat were then seen rushing down the currents of the American River. No statistics were kept regarding the number of men who lost their lives while working on the Central Pacific, but surely the figures were appalling.

Slowly, grudgingly, the white crews grew to respect the Chinese. The Chinese shared the burden of the dreaded rock work; they stuck to their own camps, never interfering with the lifestyle of the whites. As work progressed some of the Central Pacific crews became integrated. Side by side, Chinese and whites would be seen dangling from the cliffs. A Chinese worker held the sharpened rod, called a drill bit, while a white pounded it into the rock. The roles were often reversed and whites served as holders while a Chinese worker struck the bit with a hammer.

A particularly cruel winter halted progress on the Central Pacific in 1865. Crocker had hoped to continue work at least on the tunnels during the winter months, but paths leading to the tunnels were buried in snow higher than a horse's neck. It proved impossible to supply the tunneling crews. Blizzards piled snow over workers' camps to the point where only the huts' chimneys poked out. A company engineer wrote, "There were many snowslides. In some cases entire camps were carried away and the bodies of the men not found until the following spring."[6]

Spring of 1866 triggered a new effort for the Central Pacific to pierce the Sierras. A year earlier, the

The Central Pacific had to battle fierce snowstorms in the Sierra Mountains.

great Civil War had ended—the war that had stifled the efforts of the company's cross-country rival, the Union Pacific. A fortune in government money was at stake. Washington paid by the mile. Now the Union Pacific was in a position to gobble up the miles—and the money.

5

THE UNION PACIFIC MOVES WEST

We the undersigned propose to lay and fill the track of the Union Pacific Railroad . . . as fast as required . . . The track is to be laid in a workmanlike manner.[1]

—Wording from a contract signed by Jack and Dan Casement, the Union Pacific's top foremen

Groundbreaking

On a frozen December morning in 1863, a few hundred people gathered at the frontier town of Omaha, Nebraska, to witness the groundbreaking ceremony of the Union Pacific Railroad. The men and women had come by stagecoach and by boats up the Missouri River. As yet there were no railroad tracks connecting Omaha to the East. The keynote speaker was George Francis Train, an orator, a writer, and a high officer in the Union Pacific. He delivered an inspirational speech: "The great Pacific railway is commenced. . . . The Pacific railway is the nation and the nation is the Pacific railway. This is the grandest enterprise under God."[2]

Although powerful, the speech was meaningless. The Union Pacific was nowhere near prepared to begin its portion of the railroad's construction. At the time of the ceremony, the great Civil War consumed the resources of the eastern states. Supplies were short, and most able-bodied men were serving at the fighting fronts. With construction halted by war, the company concentrated on gathering money for the project ahead.

Thomas Durant, the chief of the Union Pacific, used the war years to plead for more concessions from Congress. Free spending during wartime had corrupted many members of the Senate and the House of Representatives. Congressmen, already tainted by the profits of war, now hoped to enrich themselves further when the conflict ended. Many politicians accepted free stock certificates in the Union Pacific Company. Durant also spent company money throwing lavish parties for members of Congress at Willard's Hotel in Washington, D.C. The tactics worked. In 1864, Congress doubled the already generous land grant awarded the railroads by the Pacific Railroad Act. Now the companies were given a band of land twenty miles wide—ten miles on either side of their track. By the time construction was completed, the Union Pacific alone had earned nineteen thousand square miles of free land. If put together, that much land would total more than the combined areas of Rhode Island, Vermont, and Massachusetts.

While the war raged, Durant and his fellow investors were forced to wait before they could begin building. They waited while Confederate General Robert E. Lee surrendered to Union General Ulysses S. Grant on April 9, 1865. Just five days later, the tragic news arrived that President Lincoln had been shot and killed by an assassin, John Wilkes Booth. Lincoln's body was put on a special, elaborately built railroad car for the long trip from Washington to his burial place in Springfield, Illinois. Shortly after Lincoln's burial, Thomas Durant bought the funeral car. He redecorated it and used the car as his private touring vehicle to inspect construction sites on the Union Pacific line. He often threw parties for high-ranking members of Congress in his private coach.

Throughout the Civil War years, the Union Pacific had laid not one mile of track out of Omaha. But by May 1865, it was as if the country had suffered through four years of winter and now celebrated a glorious spring. A new beginning dawned over the United States—and over the Union Pacific. Riverboats loaded with rails, spikes, and tools chugged up the Missouri to Omaha. Men gathered, too. They included ex-soldiers, ex-slaves, and immigrants from Ireland,

In this photograph, some Union Pacific executives inspect a track site.

Germany, Sweden, and a dozen other countries. The terrible war was over. Now the nation was ready to build the world's greatest railroad.

The Bosses

The Union Pacific, in sharp contrast to the Central Pacific, had an easy route to begin its task. The grasslands of Nebraska were almost monotonously flat. Nebraska and the region to the west made up the Great Plains where few hills, trees, or even shrubs broke the landscape. For thousands of years, this sea of grass supported great herds of animals. Buffalo, deer, and antelope still roamed there when the Union Pacific began work, but company officers hardly noticed the animals. The bosses wondered why the railroad was making such slow progress. Despite the flatness of the land, crews were laying only one mile of track a week.

Thomas Durant, in his zeal to lobby Congress, had failed to hire professional engineers and construction experts to spur the work forward. Instead, Durant promoted political figures to high positions in the company and hoped they would somehow supervise construction. One such political appointee was Silas Seymour, the company's acting chief engineer in the early stages. Seymour had little experience in railroad construction, but his brother was the governor of New York State. The acting chief engineer entertained some bizarre notions of how to build a railroad. He suggested the tracks be laid with crossties running parallel with the rails instead of crossing them. This would mean the rails would rest on two strips of lumber, all stretching out in the same direction with nothing to hold the rails together. When it was pointed out that rails constructed in such a manner would separate the first time a train rolled over them, Seymour defended himself by claiming that at least his idea would save on lumber. Fortunately for the railroad, Seymour's proposal was rejected.

Durant and other owners of the Union Pacific quickly realized that the company needed a change in leadership. History proved they found the proper men for the job.

In 1866, Grenville Dodge replaced Seymour as the Union Pacific's chief engineer and principal planner. Dodge was a wise choice. He had served as a general in the Civil War and had helped the North build new railroad lines. An excellent surveyor, he had already scouted the Rocky Mountains, which loomed beyond the Great Plains and posed a daunting challenge to the Union Pacific. Finally, Dodge was an experienced—and a ruthless—American Indian fighter. He had spent the better part of 1865 leading a cavalry unit against the Sioux and Cheyenne on the Great Plains. Union Pacific officials expected trouble to break out somewhere in the West.

Durant's greatest move came in 1866 when he signed on not one but two construction bosses. Jack Casement stood only five feet four inches. His brother Dan was even shorter, "five feet nothing," a friend used to say. But as bosses over a crew of tough railroad laborers, both stood ten feet tall. Workers called the brothers Jack and Dan, but never to their faces. Jack had been a Union general. Fearless under fire, he demanded strict obedience from his troops. He readily transferred his iron standards of discipline to the task of building a railroad. Several historic photos show Jack Casement overseeing construction operations with a whip in his hand.

Aside from their qualities of leadership, the Casement brothers brought innovative ideas to the construction process. Both had worked on railroad crews when they were young. They well remembered the frustration of running out of supplies while laying track. Supply breakdowns left men leaning on hammers and picks with nothing to do but wait for rails, crossties, spikes, or some other vital commodity to arrive at trackside. Worse yet, the men were collecting regular wages while they were idly waiting for supplies. The brothers vowed that their operation would not be hampered by lack of essential material. So the Casements invented the supply train. It became the heart, the soul, the brains, and the stomach of the Union Pacific's construction effort.

The supply train was pushed, never pulled, by a locomotive. Pushing the train made it easier to unload its goods. As fresh tracks were nailed down, the supply train moved steadily forward, to serve the crews. Newspaper reporters called it the perpetual train because it was always in motion. The lead car was usually a blacksmith shop on wheels. Working from flaming forges, blacksmiths made special parts to repair machinery, and they fashioned shoes for horses.

When construction reached its peak, the Union Pacific used ten thousand horses, about one for each man.

A string of other cars completed the supply train. Dining cars on the supply train featured one long table where one hundred twenty-five men ate. The men ate in shifts. To speed operations, the tin dishes were nailed to the table. That way, when one shift left the dining car, kitchen helpers needed only to swab the dishes with hand-held mops to clean them for the next shift. Although dangerously unsanitary, the nailed-down plates helped to rush workers in and out in rapid order. One car served as an office for the engineers who plotted the paths of the railroad and designed bridges, and another was a headquarters room for the bookkeepers who kept a close tab on supplies and costs. Completing the supply train were four or more cramped sleeping cars, where bunks were lined three high. Most workers slept outside in tents, shunning the barn-like sleeping quarters because they claimed the cars were infested with "cooties" (lice).

Rails were kept on flatcars on a special train which lay about a mile behind the track-laying gang. Workers put the rails on horse-drawn wagons, and drove the wagons forward to the crews. Then—with five men to each twenty-eight-foot-long, five hundred-pound rail—the rails were taken from the wagon, carried forward, and dropped onto the crossties. Using precisely

Workers often lived in camps like this one along the transcontinental railroad.

cut bars as gauges, men separated the rails so they were exactly four feet, eight and one half inches apart. This was the standard gauge for American railroads at that time. When properly spaced, the rails were spiked to the crossties by muscular men swinging sledge-hammers. A newspaper reporter gave this account of a spiking operation: "Three strokes to the spike, ten spikes to the rail, four hundred rails to the mile. Quick work, you say—but the fellows on the Union Pacific are tremendously in earnest."[3]

As the crews developed efficiency, they turned tracklaying into a symphony of muscle and metal over the Nebraska flatlands. Working together, the men managed to lay a mile a day, sometimes two miles a day. Grenville Dodge and the Casement brothers should have been pleased with the railroad building machine they had created. But instead they looked constantly west to the endless horizon. Dodge and the Casements were charged with building the longest railroad anyone had ever attempted to build, and they drove the men like beasts to complete the job.

The Civil War was still a fresh memory in 1866, when the Casement-led Union Pacific crews began their great push west. Most of the bosses had served as officers during the war. Many of the workers had marched in the ranks. It is no wonder that a military routine ruled the camps and the work process.

Working far ahead of the main gang were the surveyors, who, in military terms, could be thought of as the scouts. Often the surveyors scouted one hundred miles ahead of the main body. Next came the graders. Along the Platte River in Nebraska, the graders worked in conjunction with bridge builders who erected spans over feeder creeks leading into the Platte. Workers used the term "monkeys" to describe specialists. A man who was skilled in bridge making was called a "bridge monkey," and an expert in blasting was a "powder monkey." Finally came the infantry, the tracklayers. Slowly but steadily, the Union Pacific infantry nailed down tracks leading over the plains, while the Casement supply train hissed at their heels.

The Workers

Popular folklore says that the Irish built the Union Pacific almost by themselves. But evidence suggests that only about one third of the crews were of Irish heritage. The remaining ranks of workers were filled by Union veterans from the Midwest, ex-Confederate soldiers, and by immigrants from northern Europe who were recruited out of Chicago. As many as one thousand African Americans, many of them newly liberated slaves, worked on the project. Yet the cultural leadership of the workers was decidedly Irish. Music in the camps had an Irish beat. Middle management

Charles J. Latrobe, an English travel writer and minor poet, on "The Coming of the Irish," written in 1836:

HERE COMES A SHIPLOAD OF IRISH. . . . FROM NEW YORK THEY GO IN SWARMS TO THE CANALS, RAILROADS, AND PUBLIC WORKS, WHERE THEY PERFORM THAT LABOR WHICH THE AMERICANS ARE NOT INCLINED TO DO. NOW AND THEN THEY GET UP A FIGHT AMONG THEMSELVES IN THE STYLE OF OLD IRELAND, AND PERHAPS KILL ONE ANOTHER, EXPRESSING GREAT INDIGNATION AND SURPRISE WHEN THEY FIND THAT THEY MUST ANSWER FOR IT THOUGH THEY ARE IN A FREE COUNTRY. BY DEGREES, THE MORE THRIFTY GET AND KEEP MONEY, AND DIVING DEEPER INTO THE CONTINENT, PURCHASE LANDS; WHILE THE INTEMPERATE AND IRRECLAIMABLE VANISH FROM THE SURFACE.

THE AMERICANS COMPLAIN, AND JUSTLY, OF THE DISORDERLY POPULATION WHICH IRELAND THROWS INTO THE BOSOM OF THE UNION, BUT THERE ARE MANY REASONS WHY THEY SHOULD BE BORNE WITH. THEY, WITH THE POOR GERMANS, DO THE WORK WHICH WITHOUT THEM COULD HARDLY BE DONE.[4]

Charles J. Latrobe describes the reputations and contributions of Irish workers in America.

bosses who supervised section crews were often stout, ruddy-faced Irishmen. For many years, Irish workers had contributed to massive canal-digging and railroad-building efforts in the eastern states. The great Potato Famine of the late 1840s drove some 1.5 million impoverished Irish men and women from their island home to the United States. Many became construction laborers. When the Union Pacific advertised for workers, the Irish answered the call. Their long years of construction experience propelled them into leadership positions, and thus the myth of an Irish-built railroad was forged.

Work songs and camp ballads favored by Union Pacific gangs had their origins in Ireland: "Pat Malloy," "Brinon on the Moor," and "Poor Paddy He Works on the Railroads." Even Swedes and Finns fresh from Scandinavia mastered enough Irish-accented English words to join in these ballads. The most popular of all the company's work songs was belted out to the rhythm of driving hammers:

> *Drill, ye tarriers, drill.*
> *Drill, ye tarriers, drill.*
> *Oh, it's work all day*
> *No sugar in your tay,*
> *Workin' on the U. Pay Railway!*[5]

Laborers on the Union Pacific were paid about thirty-five dollars a month. The gangs ate meals of meat, bread, and beans, all prepared by company cooks. The meat came from herds of steer which were owned by the company and driven from camp to camp by company-paid cowboys. Although the men often grumbled about the sameness of the food, one teenage worker claimed the bread baked in supply train kitchens was the best he ever ate. Food had to be plentiful to give the men strength. Work started at about 6:30 A.M., and the crews toiled until dark.

Living and working entirely out of doors, the men had to cope with the cruelties of weather on the Great Plains. Summer brought heat and suffocating dust. Workers prayed for rain to cool things down, but when rain came it often struck like a hammer blow. With no hills or trees to bar their ferocity, prairie winds and rain screamed into the workers' camps. A Union Pacific employee named William Henry Jackson described a typical "Platte storm" that struck his crew:

> It came down raging and howling like a madman, tearing and pulling away at the [wagon] sheets as though it meant to vent its fury upon us personally. It rocked and shook us and [turned] some of the wagons over on their wheels. . . . After a short spat of hail, the rain came down in steady torrents—the roaring thunder and flashing lightning were incessant. . . . The storm did not last long, but its force and fury were indescribable.[6]

Saturday nights were occasions when Union Pacific Railroad builders could unwind from their frantic

This is an artist's drawing of a track-laying Union Pacific crew at work on the flat lands of Nebraska.

work pace. Thirty-five dollars a month was considered good pay in the 1860s. Also, with few places to spend the wages, a worker found his pockets stuffed with dollars. Early into the Union Pacific's great undertaking, hundreds of clever operators devised ways of liberating a man from his money. Every fifty miles or so a new town sprang up along the Union Pacific's path. The towns consisted entirely of saloons, gambling halls, and houses of prostitution. These establishments were housed either in tents or in hastily nailed-together shacks. When the workers of the Union Pacific laid track beyond the makeshift towns, the prostitutes and whisky merchants simply set up another settlement further along the railroad's path and waited for the crews to arrive. Thus the single track stretching westward created towns and erased them all in the course of a few months. The shifting settlements came to be called "Hell on Wheels."

While most of the Hell on Wheels towns were nameless and quickly forgotten, two such places—North Platte, Nebraska, and Julesburg, Colorado—thrive today. North Platte was winter quarters for the Union Pacific in 1866. In November of that year, its grounds were home only to prairie dogs. Then word leaked out that the railroad intended to camp there, and in three weeks North Platte had a population of one thousand. By the end of the winter, its population had increased fivefold. The British journalist Henry Stanley, who later became a famous explorer of Africa, visited North Platte and reported, "Every gambler in the Union seems to steer his course for North Platte. . . . Every house is a saloon, and every saloon is a gambling den."[7] In the spring of 1867, the Hell on Wheels town of Julesburg was born. Stanley also visited "sinful Julesburg," and watched bloody fights break out nightly in its saloons and gambling halls. He wrote, "I verily believe that there are men here who would murder a fellow creature for five dollars. Nay, there are men who have already done it. . . . Not a day

New towns and boom towns such as this one sprang up along the Union Pacific's trackside.

passes but a dead body is found somewhere in the vicinity."[8]

Winter was a frustrating time for Grenville Dodge and the Casement brothers. While winds howled and snow blanketed the Great Plains, they could do little but stockpile material for the big push in the spring. The bosses of the Union Pacific now felt a new urgency. In 1866, the company had completed more than two hundred fifty miles of track, but its officials believed that the Central Pacific was ready to break out of the Sierras and gobble up its own miles. Union Pacific owners pictured the two companies straining like track runners in starting blocks. Spring came. Bang! The great race was on.

We surely live in a very fast age;

We've traveled by ox-team, and then took the stage

But when such conveyance is all done away

We'll travel in steam cars upon the railway![1]

—From a work song favored by Mormon graders who toiled for the Union Pacific

THE GREAT RACE

The Central Pacific—Setbacks in the West

In California, Charles Crocker fumed. For months his workers had hacked at rock trying to dig the Summit Tunnel through the toughest mountain of the Sierras. The tunnel had to be twenty feet high and more than fifteen hundred feet long before it broke out on the eastern side of the mountain. The agonizing work involved thousands of men and so far had resulted in only a few feet of tunnel. The mountain was solid granite. Workers pounded drill bits into its side to create holes for blasting powder. Very often, however, the blast simply shot back out of the hole, hardly loosening the rock at all. While the Union Pacific was leaping ahead a mile or so each day, the Central Pacific measured its daily progress in inches.

Clearly, the company needed a more powerful explosive than the blasting powder then in use. Dynamite had been invented, but few engineers in California had ever even seen the new product. Nitroglycerin was available. However, crews were terrified of nitroglycerin because the material was known to explode if simply exposed to heat or if given even a gentle thump. In April 1866, a keg of nitroglycerin slated to go to the Central Pacific blew up in a San Francisco warehouse, killing a dozen people and causing panic in the city. In another blasting mishap, the Central Pacific's foreman, James Strobridge, lost an eye to a flying rock splinter. Being half blind did not slow Strobridge at all, however. Wearing an eyepatch, he continued to scream at his crew when he was displeased with their work pace. The Chinese laborers who had mastered a few words of English called Strobridge "One-Eye Bossy Man."

Despite its instability, nitroglycerin was employed extensively to blast through the Summit Tunnel. It was used the same way as blasting powder—by drilling holes into the mountain's face, inserting the nitroglycerin, and blasting the mountain into loose stones. When nitroglycerin worked properly, it was a spectacular explosive. But no one knows how many lives or limbs were lost in nitroglycerin accidents.

The use of a mighty explosive failed to satisfy Charles Crocker. Work on the Summit Tunnel was still painfully slow. He feared the Union Pacific would be in California by the time his men completed the long bore through the peak. So Crocker made a momentous decision. First, he left an eight-thousand-worker crew on the western side of the mountain and ordered them to chisel away at the tunnel in round-the-clock twelve-hour shifts. Then, in the spring of 1867, while snow still covered the Sierras, Crocker and three thousand Chinese laborers pushed tons of equipment up one side of the mountain and down the far side. The move meant that everything the men needed in order to work—from sacks of potatoes to kegs of nails—had to be carried over a seven-thousand-foot-high peak. Crews even dismantled a locomotive and forty railroad cars and carted them over the snow-covered range. The men fashioned sleighs out of logs and hitched the sleighs to huge teams of horses to accomplish this fantastic moving job.

On the eastern side of the mountains, Crocker split up his crew. With half the men he formed a tunneling party and directed it to bore westward into the mountain on a precise course designed to meet the main gang coming from the other side. The second

This photograph shows a portion of the Summit Tunnel, the Central Pacific's toughest challenge.

half of his crew began tracklaying on the relatively flat land approaching Nevada. Crocker set a goal to complete at least one mile of track a day. More than a year passed before the Summit Tunnel was complete to the point of allowing trains to pass through, but Crocker was determined to begin the tracklaying process west of the Sierras. Crocker knew that in the spring of 1867 the Union Pacific was poised to make rapid progress on the flat lands of the Great Plains. The Central Pacific boss feared that his company was doomed to be the tortoise—the painfully slow runner—in this tortoise-and-hare race.

War on the Plains

Few of the Sioux and Cheyenne peoples who lived on the Great Plains had ever seen railroad tracks or locomotives before the coming of Union Pacific work gangs. Yet the Plains peoples guessed—rightly, it turned out—that the thundering and hissing Iron Horses would mark the final end for their way of life. They knew that wherever the railroad went, hordes of white settlers followed, and that settlers habitually crowded the American Indians out of their ancient lands.

Still, the initial contact between the American Indians and Union Pacific crews was cordial. In 1866, a band of Sioux, led by a feared chief named Spotted

This is one of the hastily constructed depot towns that developed along the Central Pacific line.

Tail, approached a grading gang working on the plains. The Sioux wanted to trade goods. The graders invited them to share their lunch. Everyone ate in good spirits. After lunch, the whites requested a demonstration of Sioux skill with the bow and arrow. A Union Pacific grader leaned a shovel against a wagon. Standing about sixty feet away, one Sioux after another shot an arrow through the shovel's hand grip. The whites were stunned by the demonstration.

Peace did not last long, however. The American Indians quickly became infuriated over invasion by the railroad. Months after their first contact, the Sioux attempted to attack a Union Pacific train. Sioux warriors knew the Iron Horses were fast because on several occasions they tried to race a train on their ponies. But they had no idea of a locomotive's power. Tragedy resulted when a band of about fifty warriors determined they could stop a train by holding a rawhide rope across the tracks. The train approached at about twenty-five miles an hour. Possibly the engineer grinned when he saw the men take up tug-of-war positions on either side of the track. The Iron Horse roared into the rope at full steam, and the Sioux were dashed about like toy dolls. Those closest to the tracks were cut to pieces under the train wheels. The Sioux learned the power of the Iron Horse and never again tried a stunt so foolish.

Through much of 1867, a war raged between the Union Pacific and the Plains peoples. The railroad had the advantage during the conflict. Mostly the whites worked in huge crews of a thousand or more men. A large percentage of the workers were Civil War veterans. At a signal, the men dropped their shovels and hammers, picked up rifles, and formed a skirmish line just as they used to do in wartime. Sioux and Cheyenne bands shied away from attacking these large, well-armed crews.

But trains and small gangs of Union Pacific workers came under ferocious assaults. One of the deadliest of such battles occurred near Plum Creek, Nebraska, in August 1867. Led by a chief named Turkey Leg, a war party of Cheyennes lashed surplus crossties onto tracks with wire and waited for a train to approach. It was night when a train with a six-man crew aboard chugged toward the barricade. Unable to see the obstruction, the Iron Horse crashed into the ties and derailed. The Cheyenne swarmed upon the railroad men, and in seconds killed five of the six. The only white man still alive was a young Englishman named William Thompson. He escaped, but his flight from Plum Creek turned into an odyssey.

Thompson had been thrown from the train when it crashed. He rose to his hands and knees, dazed, but able to understand his terrible peril. For years he had worn his blond hair so long that it fell down to his shoulders. Suddenly he felt a violent tug on his hair. This was followed by a surge of searing, unbearable pain on the side of his head. Through his tears and agony he looked up to see a Cheyenne warrior walking away holding a handful of his hair with a bloody patch of scalp attached to it. Thompson had been scalped, and had somehow lived through the ordeal. He decided to play dead, thinking this ploy was his only hope for survival. As he lay in the dirt, Thompson saw the Cheyenne tie the scalp to his belt in order to take it home as a prize of war. But, unnoticed by the attacker, the scalp fell to the ground. Thompson lay still, waiting.

The Cheyenne war party attacked another train that night, looting it and killing two men. Meanwhile, William Thompson crawled forward, picked up his scalp, and stuffed it into his pocket. He reasoned that perhaps a doctor could sew it back onto his head if he ever managed to reach civilization again. Before dawn he had hobbled to the Plum Creek station, his head covered with blood. There Thompson was put on a train to Omaha, some two hundred fifty miles away. A doctor treated his head wound, but was unable to reattach the scalp. Though Thompson retained an ugly scar on his head, he lived long enough to be a grandfather. Eventually the scalp was given to the

Omaha Public Library, where it was displayed under glass for the next one hundred years as a ghastly example of the Union Pacific's war with the Plains peoples.

To protect the railroad, Washington officials ordered the United States Cavalry onto the Great Plains. By 1868 more than five thousand soldiers were patrolling the railroad and its projected path. Leading the contingent was General William Tecumseh Sherman. His attitude toward American Indians was revealed in his often quoted statement, "The only good Indians I ever saw were dead."[2] Sherman, a friend of Grenville Dodge, kept the Plains peoples at bay while work on the railroad continued. The general ordered his troops to attack if they saw even a small hunting party. Sherman wrote at the time, "The more we can kill this year, the less will have to be killed the next war, for the more I see of these Indians the more convinced I am that they all have to be killed or be maintained as a species of paupers."[3]

The Plains peoples survived by avoiding direct conflict with the cavalry. Instead, they waged a hit-and-run war against railroad property, tearing up tracks and burning supply sheds. Often they chopped down the telegraph poles that paralleled the tracks, and stripped them of what they called the "talking wires." But the guerrilla warfare tactics served only to slow down the

The railroad often had problems with American Indians as it continued to build through their traditional lands. Here, Union Pacific officers are negotiating with leaders of the Plains tribes.

progress of the Union Pacific. Durant, Dodge, and the Casement brothers had expected to complete 288 miles of track in 1867; the Indian Wars limited that number to 245.

True to American Indian fears, the railroad eroded their way of life by drawing settlers to the Great Plains. After a little more than a year, hundreds of farms and a score of towns had grown along the Union Pacific's tracks. The population of Nebraska jumped fivefold, to more than a hundred thousand, and the territory became a state in 1867. The settlers killed buffalo, the primary source of food for the Plains peoples. Pioneers from the East also built barbed wire fences that disturbed the buffalo's grazing patterns. The reduction of the great buffalo herds doomed the lifestyle that the Sioux and other peoples had enjoyed for centuries.

Frustration and Promise

On the western side of the country, Charles Crocker had little trouble with American Indians. When curious American Indians hung around the camps, Crocker hired them. The Central Pacific was always short of labor, and Crocker would take on anyone willing to work.

The American Indians employed by the Central Pacific worked easily with the Chinese. In fact, friendships developed. At night the two peoples spoke through interpreters and exchanged stories over campfires. The stories led to their only problem. One evening, a Paiute storyteller told a group of Chinese that in the desert lands beyond the mountains lurked snakes so big that they could swallow a man in one horrible gulp. The next morning, Charles Crocker woke to discover that five hundred Chinese laborers had broken camp and were now hurrying back to Sacramento. Crocker rode out to intercept the Chinese and persuade them that no such gargantuan snakes existed anywhere in America. The Chinese returned, but Crocker spent weeks cursing the Paiutes for their love of tall tales.

Despite their multicultural nature, the Central Pacific's work camps were peaceful. Squabbles between the Chinese and whites were few. Strobridge, the Irish-born construction foreman who had first opposed hiring Chinese, had learned to like them. Said Strobridge, "They learn quickly, do not fight, have no strikes that amount to anything, and are very cleanly in their habits. They will gamble and do quarrel among themselves most noisily—but harmlessly."[4]

But while a degree of racial harmony prevailed among the construction crews, the people of California posed another problem. Lured by railroad jobs, thousands of Chinese poured into California from their native land. While the bulk of the immigrants headed inland for construction sites, many established small businesses in San Francisco and Sacramento. By 1867 the Chinese population of California had topped one hundred thousand. In March of that year, angry whites formed the Anti-Coolie Labor Association. Leaders of the organization insisted that low-paid Chinese workers—called coolies—would depress wages everywhere in the state. Mobs of Chinese-hating Californians, many of them drinking from whisky bottles, roamed city streets throwing rocks at immigrants and torching Chinese laundries. So many Chinese were beaten up and killed that a new expression—"not a Chinaman's chance"—entered the English language. The expression meant that the odds of a Chinese immigrant preserving his life in a California city were slim.

Some whites were outraged by California's treatment of the Chinese newcomers. A white minister observed fellow whites bullying Chinese and wrote:

> The San Francisco hoodlum is notorious. [Hoodlums] follow the Chinaman through the streets, howling and screaming after him to frighten him. They catch hold of his cue [pigtail] and pull him from wagons. They throw brickbats [bricks] and missiles at him. Sometimes the police have made a show of protecting the Chinaman, but too frequently the effort has been a heartless one.[5]

Excerpt from the Chinese Exclusion Act, May 6, 1882:

WHEREAS, IN THE OPINION OF THE GOVERNMENT OF THE UNITED STATES THE COMING OF CHINESE LABORERS TO THIS COUNTRY ENDANGERS THE GOOD ORDER OF CERTAIN LOCALITIES WITHIN THE TERRITORY THEREOF: THEREFORE,

BE IT ENACTED, THAT FROM AND AFTER THE EXPIRATION OF NINETY DAYS NEXT AFTER THE PASSAGE OF THIS ACT . . . THE COMING OF CHINESE LABORERS TO THE UNITED STATES BE, . . . SUSPENDED; AND DURING SUCH SUSPENSION IT SHALL NOT BE LAWFUL FOR ANY CHINESE LABORER TO COME, OR, HAVING SO COME AFTER THE EXPIRATION OF SAID NINETY DAYS, TO REMAIN WITHIN THE UNITED STATES. [6]

Chinese laborers on the transcontinental railroad often faced discrimination and even violence from whites in California. By 1882, after the completion of the railroad, the hostility toward the Chinese had become so strong that the United States government passed the Chinese Exclusion Act, to prevent Chinese from living and working in America.

But sympathetic whites, like the minister, could do little more than complain about anti-Chinese brutality in California.

Over the winter of 1867–1868, the Union Pacific's tracks poked into Wyoming and created the new Hell on Wheels town of Cheyenne. Like its predecessors, Cheyenne was both a boom town and a den of vice. One newspaper writer reported, "Lots in this desert city ran up from nothing to five thousand dollars in five days; there was a great scramble for them." The same writer added, "The population [of Cheyenne] is of that rough, uncouth kind. . . . Looking down its street, upon which nearly the whole town is built, we see whisky and beer shops. . . . 'Firewater' is a big thing in this country."[7]

Breaking out of the Great Plains, the Union Pacific now labored in desert country east of the Rocky Mountains. Water was always in short supply, but the going was comparatively smooth. In the distance loomed the towering Rockies, the same type of rugged terrain that had so far hampered the Central Pacific. At the end of 1867, the Union Pacific had completed 540 miles of track from Omaha. By comparison, the Central Pacific's progress totaled only 131 miles out of Sacramento. But Central Pacific officers looked upon 1868 as a breakthrough year. By June of that year, the tunnel system would be complete through the Sierras,

The Union Pacific celebrates reaching the "100th Meridian," a point 247 miles from Omaha.

allowing great quantities of supplies to be brought forward on trains. Now, said the Big Four, was the time for record progress.

The country buzzed with excitement as Americans everywhere envisioned a historic linkup between the two companies. Newspaper writers reported every fresh mile of track. Reporters who camped with advance crews wrote that they worked at "the front," as if they were on a field of war. From New York to San Francisco, Americans made bets as to which company would cover the most ground. The transcontinental railroad was the grandest story since Robert E. Lee's surrender, which ended the Civil War.

Down the stretch came the great race. In the American mind it pitted East against West and Irish against Chinese. It was said that the Union Pacific ran on whisky, while the Central Pacific ran on tea.

No sooner did trains begin to arrive from Sacramento with their loads of freight and passengers than Reno began to bustle with life.[1]

—A newspaper account of how the Central Pacific's newly laid tracks caused the birth of Reno, Nevada

PROMONTORY

Waste for the Sake of Speed

Mormons working for the Central Pacific were a sharp contrast to the Irish who toiled for the Union Pacific. Mormons did not drink or use tobacco. They did not even swear. Yet the Irish claimed the Mormons lived in sin because many of them had more than one wife. Despite their differences, the Irish and Mormons worked together building the transcontinental railroad. The massive construction project had a way of uniting widely diverse cultures.

Led by the energetic Brigham Young, the Mormons had arrived in Utah in 1847. Their practice of polygamy—allowing a man to take more than one wife—had caused outraged neighbors to brutally push them out of their previous settlements in Missouri and Illinois. The members of the religious sect then trekked westward and found their Promised Land in Utah's Great Salt Lake Valley. By the late 1860s, the Mormons were the only large group in the West that the railroads could call upon when they needed additional workers.

Although Mormon society was religious in nature, its leader Brigham Young was not averse to making money. He signed a $2 million contract with Thomas Durant and the Union Pacific to have Mormon crews build a track grade across much of Utah. Then the Central Pacific entered Utah from the west, and Young signed a similar contract with the Big Four. As a result, Mormon crews built two paths for the tracks, even though Young and other Mormon leaders knew that only one of the paths would be used. Later, the unused grade served only to collect weeds. Still, both the Mormons and the railroads made money. Such was the wastefulness generated by the great race.

One thriftless practice piled onto another as the companies drew nearer. Cuts were expensive and time-consuming to build. Therefore cuts were ignored, and crews laid tracks in giant loops around hills rather than through them. Both companies took the attitude, "What the heck, the government's paying by the mile." Years later, the twisting tracks had to be torn up and straightened out. To save time and money, the builders started making their crossties out of soft pine instead of hardwood such as oak, as was specified in the government contracts. After just a few months' use, the pine crossties caved in under the weight of trains and many thousands of ties had to be replaced. Bridges along the route were shoddily constructed. Some bridges even swayed in strong winds. An 1869 traveler on the Union Pacific's portion of the railway wrote:

> A bridge [was] built upon [a base] of soft sandstone [and] crumbled away under our train. . . . One passenger was killed and several more or less injured . . . The bridge as well as two others in the vicinity had been examined the day previous and pronounced unsafe.[2]

Washington's reluctance to set a goal for the two companies encouraged further waste. The original 1862 Pacific Railroad Act forbade the Central Pacific from building beyond the Sierra Nevada. This position was dropped when the Central Pacific pointed out that the restriction left them unable to make as much money as could their rivals in the East. So authorities in Washington, D.C., told the companies that they could build until they met. However, when the construction crews entered Utah, Congress could not agree upon a proper rendezvous spot. Consequently, the companies continued grading until their crews overlapped and were working on parallel paths for track. At some points the work gangs were so close that the men, who by this time were caught up in the competition, exchanged jeers and curses. Insults escalated into fistfights. Soon rival crews blasted each other's roadbeds with explosives, burying several workers.

Finally, Washington settled the matter on April 10, 1869, by passing a joint resolution: "Resolved: that the common terminus of the Union Pacific and the Central Pacific railroads shall be at or near Ogden [Utah]."[3] Engineers for the companies then worked out an exact meeting point. They chose a dusty, sagebrush-covered plain in Utah's Promontory Mountains and named it, for the occasion, Promontory Point.

The Race within a Race

During 1868, the last full year of construction, the Central Pacific completed 360 miles of track, while the Union Pacific built 425 miles. Both records were astounding. Crews from the East as well as the West had developed such artistic perfection that their tracklaying could be compared to a ballet. Working in precise order, men spaced crossties on a track bed. Then, coming only seconds behind, another team dropped rails on the ties. Gaugers separated the tracks the proper width. Finally, a crew spiked the rails home.

This is the eastern exit of the Summit Tunnel through the Sierra Mountains.

Not a minute nor a motion was wasted in this magnificently ordered dance. One reporter called the track-laying process "a grand anvil chorus."[4]

Pride in this marvelous workmanship led to boasts. The most outrageous boast came from Charles Crocker, who claimed his Central Pacific men could lay ten miles of track in one day. Impossible, cried Thomas Durant of the Union Pacific. On a good day, Union Pacific crews could build four miles of track. On one occasion—in a demonstration deliberately designed to embarrass the Central Pacific—Durant's men completed eight miles in a one-day shift. But ten miles of track in a day? No human beings could do that, insisted Durant. Crocker bet the Union Pacific boss that his men could accomplish the feat. Ten thousand dollars, said Crocker, put up or shut up. Durant accepted the wager.

The great ten-mile attempt came on April 28, 1869. Crocker and Strobridge were ready. Five supply trains carrying rails, crossties, spikes, food, water, and everything else needed for the big push rested on the tracks. More than eight hundred fifty men, a hand-picked crew of Chinese and Irish workers, waited. At the time, the railheads of the Central Pacific and the Union Pacific were less than thirty miles apart. Officials from the Union Pacific, including Durant, Grenville Dodge, and the Casement brothers, were

This is a view of Pleasant Valley in Nevada. In this flat land, construction problems eased for the Central Pacific.

present to watch. Durant hoped to call Crocker's bluff and to collect money from the wager. Newspaper reporters were there, too. The horse-race efforts to build a Pacific railroad made headlines everywhere, and this race within a race was the latest chapter in the exciting story.

At 7:00 A.M., a whistle from the Central Pacific supply train howled, signaling the start. The crew sprang into action. Chinese laborers brought crossties and rails forward. A reporter for *The San Francisco Bulletin* wrote, "In eight minutes, the sixteen cars [of the first supply train] were cleared with a noise like the bombardment of an army."[5] Gaugers spaced the rails and workers swinging sledgehammers spiked them into crossties. The sound of steel rang over the mountains like a chorus of church bells. Chinese and Irish worked together in magnificent concert. An army officer who was present said, "It was just like an army marching over the ground and leaving tracks behind them."

Still, Thomas Durant scoffed at the idea that this crew—or any other crew—could complete ten miles of track in one shift. The very notion seemed laughable.

Throughout the morning the brutal work pace continued. *The San Francisco Bulletin* reporter wrote:

> The scene was an animated one. There was a line of men advancing a mile an hour; iron cars with their load of rails and humans dashed up and down the

newly-laid track; foremen on horseback were galloping back and forth. . . . Alongside the moving force, teams were hauling food and water wagons. Chinamen with pails dangling from poles balanced over their shoulders were moving among the men with water and tea.[6]

At 1:30 P.M., a train whistle blew, announcing a break for lunch. By the break the men of the Central Pacific had laid more than six miles of track. Already a supply train waited on the fresh track with goods needed to complete the final four miles. Durant ate lunch nervously, fearing he would lose his bet. Crocker, on the other hand, laughed as he munched his food. A writer from the *Alta California* said, "[Crocker's] merry laugh was heard all day along the line."[7]

Crocker had reason to laugh. By the end of the twelve-hour shift, his men had built a stretch of track measuring ten miles and fifty-six feet. Never before had railroad workers constructed so much ready-to-use track in a single day. A spectator with a head for figures calculated that in this one Herculean effort the Central Pacific crew consumed 3,520 rails, 25,800 ties, and 28,160 spikes. Crocker collected his ten-thousand-dollar bet from Durant, and graciously shook hands with his men. In those days, ten thousand dollars was more than the average railroad worker could earn in twenty years. Whether or not Crocker gave his men a tip is unknown.

This artist's drawing shows work on the last mile of the transcontinental railroad, and the sometimes painful meeting of white and Chinese workers.

The Last Spike

May 10, 1869. Jubilation! All the tracks on the Pacific Railroad were finished, except for a few feet of connecting rails to be laid this glorious day. The final tally stood: The Union Pacific had laid 1,085 miles of track from Promontory Point east to Omaha, and the Central Pacific had built 690 miles stretching west from Promontory to Sacramento. The colossal effort had taken three and one half years, starting from the end of the Civil War when work really heated up to the final completion in the spring of 1869. Experts disagree as to how much the two companies received from the federal government in cash payments and in land grants, but the final total was considerable. The Central Pacific collected just about as much money in government subsidies as did its rival, because its route ran over so much mountainous terrain. In all, some 1,775 hard miles were completed to link Omaha with Sacramento. Now, finally, at Promontory Point, East was poised to shake hands with West. Certainly this was the time for celebration.

All over the country, Americans waited to hear word by telegraph that the final spike had been driven. The great Pacific Railroad marked the ultimate triumph of manifest destiny. At last a gleaming iron track had tied the country together from the Atlantic shores to the Pacific. Church leaders praised the railroad as a miracle granted to America by God.

All was not rosy, however. The ceremony had to be delayed for several days because the Union Pacific experienced what was called "labor trouble." On May 6, 1869, a private railroad car carrying Thomas Durant and other high-ranking Union Pacific officers pulled into the station at Piedmont, Wyoming. The car was greeted by a mob of angry workers, many of whom carried rifles. "Doctor" Thomas Durant, always a slippery operator, had missed several paydays. He told the workers that accounting errors were at fault, and said they would soon get their wages. But with the project almost finished, the workers would accept no excuses. The men switched Durant's car to a siding and chained the wheels to the tracks. Thus kidnapped, Durant had no other choice but to grant the pay. He wired for the money to be brought up on a special train. Some reports claim the back pay totaled more than $250,000. Once paid, the men freed their boss. The golden spike ceremony could then continue.

Monday morning, May 10, was a perfect day, sunny with a bit of chill in the air. A crowd gathered at Promontory Point. Although it was early in the morning, many men and women were already drinking champagne. Two golden spikes and two silver ones were to be placed at the ties that day. Leading figures slated to pound the spikes home were Leland Stanford of the Central Pacific, and Thomas Durant of the Union Pacific. "Pound" was hardly a proper word to describe the process. Holes had already been drilled into the crossties. All one had to do was to drop the spike into the hole and tap it with a very light hammer. Such ceremonial spikes marked the completion of many railroads. They never stayed in the tracks. Instead, they were quickly removed and replaced by standard spikes. The famous gold spike that Leland Stanford inserted is now displayed at the Stanford Museum of Stanford University in California.

Speeches—many of them long-winded—were given by railroad officials and by politicians. One witness recalled, "I do not remember what any of the speakers said now, but I do remember there was a great abundance of champagne."[8] At one point champagne flowed so freely that celebrants poured it over the two train engines. Charles Crocker limited his speech to five minutes, and to his credit, praised his Chinese workers:

> I wish to call to mind in the midst of our rejoicing that the early completion of this railroad we have built has been in great measure due to that poor, destitute class of laborers called the Chinese—to the fidelity and industry they have shown.[9]

The last two rails were placed on ties—one by an Irish Union Pacific crew, and another by Chinese workers of the Central Pacific. Only one mishap occurred. A photographer pointed his camera at the Chinese, and his assistant shouted something like, "Now's the time to take a shot." Many of the Chinese had never seen a camera before, and they had limited knowledge of English. They did, however, understand the word "shot." The word caused them to drop the rail and rush into the sagebrush. Only the assurances of trusted officials such as Crocker convinced them to come back and finish the job.

The climactic moment in the ceremony was to come with Leland Stanford's initial blow on the line's final spike. This was an iron spike, the gold one having already been stashed away. Hoping to thrill the country, an engineer had attached one telegraph wire to the head of Stanford's sledgehammer and another to the spike. That way, the instant that spike and hammer made contact, a telegraph signal would be sent throughout the United States heralding the completion of the great railroad. Thus wired, Leland Stanford poised above the spike. He drew the hammer over his head and swung. And he missed!

"What a howl went up!" said a witness, Alexander Toponce. "Irish, Chinese, Mexicans and everybody yelled with delight. 'He missed it! Yee!' The train engineers blew their whistles and rang their bells."[10]

Jubilation! This famous photograph was taken as the two trains touched together, marking the completion of the transcontinental railroad.

On the second try, Stanford hit the mark. The blow was an anticlimax because a telegraph operator, frustrated by watching Stanford's clumsy efforts, had already clicked out an excited message: "DONE!" The words triggered a nationwide party, like the Fourth of July coming in early May. At Promontory Point, the two engines—*Jupiter* and *No. 119*—chugged forward until their pilots gently touched. In San Francisco, the ceremony inspired Bret Harte to pen his poem:

What was it the Engines said,
Pilots touching,—head to head.
Facing on a single track,
Half a world behind each back?

Said the Engine from the West:
"I am from Sierra's crest;
And if altitude's a test,
Why, I reckon it's confessed
That I've done my level best."

Said the Engine from the East:
"They who work best talk the least.
S'pose you whistle down your brakes;
What you've done is no great shakes,—
Pretty fair,—but let our meeting
Be a different kind of greeting.
Let those folks with champagne stuffing,
Not their Engines, do the puffing . . ."

That is what the Engines said,
Unreported and unread;
Spoken slightly through the nose,
With a whistle at the close.[11]

May God continue the unity of our country as this railroad unites the two great oceans of the world.[1]

—The prayer engraved on the golden spike which, symbolically, marked the completion of the transcontinental railroad

RAILS WEST

Passengers

Just five days after the golden spike celebration, regular service began on the Pacific Railroad. Once a day passengers climbed aboard trains at Omaha for the trip west, and similarly a daily train left Sacramento bound for the East. Since the railway consisted only of a single track, one train had to wait at designated sidings to allow the other to pass. Head-on accidents were avoided due to slow-moving trains and careful schedules.

The trip from Omaha to Sacramento took an express train about four and one-half days. Old-time 49ers considered this speed to be astonishing, since they remembered taking a grueling six-month trip to complete their westward journey. Through connecting lines, a person could board a train in New York City and arrive in San Francisco in a little over a week. A

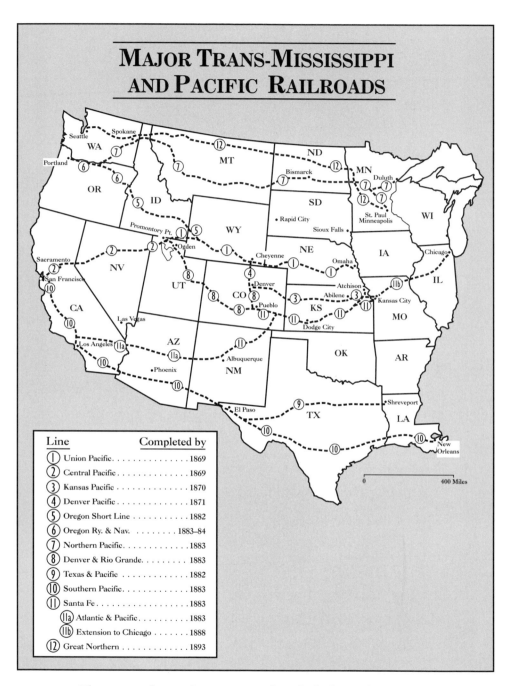

MAJOR TRANS-MISSISSIPPI AND PACIFIC RAILROADS

Line	Completed by
① Union Pacific	1869
② Central Pacific	1869
③ Kansas Pacific	1870
④ Denver Pacific	1871
⑤ Oregon Short Line	1882
⑥ Oregon Ry. & Nav.	1883–84
⑦ Northern Pacific	1883
⑧ Denver & Rio Grande	1883
⑨ Texas & Pacific	1882
⑩ Southern Pacific	1883
⑪ Santa Fe	1883
⑪ₐ Atlantic & Pacific	1883
⑪ᵦ Extension to Chicago	1888
⑫ Great Northern	1893

This map shows the major railroads linking the eastern United States to the West, and the dates of their completion.

cross-country traveler had to change trains at points such as Chicago and Omaha, but the ability to ride coast to coast on shining silver rails seemed like a miracle.

Omaha to Sacramento was the most popular run. In 1870, the first full year of operation, more than one hundred fifty thousand people bought tickets for the thrilling journey. Tickets were sold in first class, which cost a hundred dollars and included a hinged seat which was made into a bed, and second class, costing eighty dollars but without a bed. A third-class ticket cost forty dollars and was favored by farm families hoping to get a fresh start in the West. Third-class passengers rode on non-express trains which carried mainly freight, and were often forced to wait long hours on sidings to allow the passage of swift express runs. In those days a well-to-do banker earned about a hundred dollars a month. Therefore, the price of a ticket was costly. No matter. People even went into debt for the privilege of crossing the country on a magnificent Iron Horse. Railroad companies had to turn away would-be ticket buyers because they lacked space in the cars.

The most excited passengers were those from the eastern states venturing west for the first time. Out of Omaha they saw prairie land, unbroken to the horizon. Easterners likened the Great Plains to the sea on a calm day. Indeed, when wind ruffled prairie grasses the effect looked like rolling waves. From train windows they stared transfixed at animals they had never seen before. Prairie dogs scurried about in their villages. Fleet antelopes outraced the train. Travelers also saw elk, wolves, and bears. Few buffalo remained on the Union Pacific route, but for senseless sport passengers shot rifles from train windows, slaughtering the buffalo they observed. The trains' top speed in the early 1870s was about thirty-five miles per hour; the average speed was much lower. While this pace afforded a leisurely look at the animals, it seemed terrifyingly fast to most passengers.

Many people from the East longed to see genuine live American Indians. The Easterners were usually disappointed. The majority of Plains peoples hated the Iron Horse and avoided its tracks. The few Sioux and Cheyenne who did venture near the stations were hardly the "noble savages" the Easterners had imagined. American Indians seen at the stations had run out of the will to fight, and instead came to beg or to sell cheap souvenirs.

The Rocky Mountains offered a spectacular change of scenery for the westward-bound traveler. "Grand beyond description," wrote one Union Pacific customer. "[I see] castles in the air . . . fantastic shapes and profiles."[2] Here the train passed through tunnels and incredible synthetic canyons. In the Rockies, passengers came to grips with the sheer enormity of the construction project.

Comfort on the four- to five-day run depended on one's ticket. Some cars in luxurious first class had an organ or a piano where passengers gathered around at night to sing songs. The instrument was played by the conductor or by a volunteer passenger. The fanciest cars were provided by the Pullman Company of Chicago. Splendid Pullman Palace Cars were graced with fine wood paneling, upholstered seats, and beds. Second-class cars offered comfortable seating, but the passengers were forced to curl up on their seats and try to sleep during the long journey. Third-class accommodations were limited to rows of wooden benches. Aside from sightseeing, passengers of all classes passed the time by reading or playing cards. First-class cars had their own well-stocked libraries. Many people wrote letters home as they rolled along. Veteran western travelers, accustomed to bumpy stagecoaches, marveled at the fact that they could actually write on a piece of paper as the miles slipped by. On Sundays the railroads offered church services on the move for all ticket holders.

Finding something to eat was a problem regardless of one's ticket. A dining car operated on a special train run by the Pullman Company. But that train, which

This is an advertisement appealing for passengers to ride on the great Pacific Railroad.

was reserved for the super wealthy, ran only once a week. The rest of the time passengers had to grab a meal during thirty-minute stops at stations. Food there was dreary and over-priced. Isabella Lucy Bird, an Englishwoman who rode the transcontinental railroad in 1873, said the stations offered "coarse, greasy meals, infested by lazy flies."[3] A traveler from Cleveland was surprised that in the station at Sidney, Nebraska, he was served "an excellent breakfast—a chicken stew." He was later informed the stew was made not from chickens, but from prairie dogs—"a new variety of chickens," he lamented, "without feathers."[4]

Winter was the scourge of the cross-country traveler. Legendary snowfalls in the Sierras covered the tracks to the point where only the tops of telegraph poles poked up. The Central Pacific tried to clear its tracks with the aid of a special snowplow train. The plow train had a huge iron wedge which looked like the forward part of a ship's hull attached to its front end. But even the full power of the Iron Horse pushing the plow failed to cut a path through the heaviest snows. Snowbound passengers had to wait in their train for hours and sometimes even days. Fortunately, wood-burning stoves kept the cars warm. In a desperate measure, the Central Pacific covered the snowiest sections of its tracks with long wooden sheds. Some forty miles of such sheds were built in the

Sierras. The solution, however, created a problem. The sheds could not be removed in the summer, and passengers complained they were unable to behold the spectacular mountain vistas. Responding to their complaints, the Central Pacific cut long windows on both sides of the sheds. Passengers were then presented with a limited panorama from the train windows, almost like a movie.

The threat of train robberies added to the passengers' worries. In November 1870, six men boarded the Central Pacific Express at Truckee, California, and an hour later held guns on the engineer, demanding that he stop the train. The men then robbed everyone in the first-class cars, and took the payroll for a large company—a total of forty thousand dollars in loot. No one ever found out the names of those Central Pacific hijackers. Other robbers who plundered the western rails became storied outlaws: Sam Bass, Dutch Charlie Burris, Big Nose George Parrot, and the most infamous of all, Jesse James.

The letters and reports of early cross-country train riders contain complaints, but they are also filled with awe. Americans swelled with pride because the three-thousand-mile length of their country was now banded together by a metal belt of tracks. The Civil War had torn the country asunder; the transcontinental railroad

Central Pacific crews build snow cover sheds.

mended its wounds. Crews had punched holes in mountains, spanned rivers with bridges, and battled American Indian warriors. The construction project that once seemed to be a fool's dream became an iron reality. Americans were certain that no other nation on earth possessed the genius to produce such a wonder as their Pacific Railroad.

Thirty years after the first transcontinental railroad was completed, four more such lines spanned the West. No longer would a Westerner feel out of touch and isolated from the rest of the nation. More than any other institution, the railroads developed the West, cementing the American vision of manifest destiny. It is no wonder that the western railroads were the subject of songs, poetry, and stories. One such poem was written by the American master, Walt Whitman:

> *I see over my own continent the Pacific Railroad*
> *   surmounting every barrier,*
> *I see continual trains of cars winding along the*
> *   Platte carrying freight and passengers,*
> *I hear locomotives rushing and roaring, and the*
> *   shrill steam-whistle,*
> *I hear the echoes reverberate through the grandest*
> *   scenery in the world . . .*
> *I see the clear waters of lake Tahoe, I see forests of*
> *   majestic pines . . .*
> *Marking through these and after all, in duplicate*
> *   lender lines . . .*
> *Tying the Eastern to the Western sea . . .*[5]

★ TIMELINE ★

Early 1840s—A spirit of manifest destiny (westward expansion) grips the United States.

1848—Gold is discovered on Johann Sutter's property in Sacramento, California.

1849—Some eighty-five thousand gold seekers (later called 49ers) flock to California.

1854—Railroads coming from the eastern states reach Rock Island, Illinois, on the banks of the Mississippi River.

1855—Congress evaluates possible routes for a Pacific railroad.

1860—Abraham Lincoln is elected president; the election infuriates the Southern states.

1861—*April 12:* The Civil War begins when South Carolina opens fire on Fort Sumter.

1861—*April 30:* The Central Pacific Railroad Company of California is formed.

1862—*July 1:* President Lincoln signs the Pacific Railway Act, which sets the route for a transcontinental railroad and authorizes two companies to build tracks.

1862—*September 2:* The Union Pacific Railroad and Telegraph Company is created.

1863—*January 8:* Groundbreaking ceremony for the Central Pacific takes place in Sacramento; the ceremony is meaningless because the company is not prepared to begin construction.

1863—*November 2:* Theodore Judah, the inspirational leader of the transcontinental railroad, dies of yellow fever.

1863—*December 2:* The Union Pacific holds its groundbreaking ceremony in Omaha, but it, too, is woefully unprepared to begin construction.

1864—Over the summer months, workers on the Central Pacific complete the Bloomer Cut near Newcastle, California; it is the first of many large synthetic canyons the company had to build in the Sierra Nevada region.

1865—*Spring:* Charles Crocker of the Central Pacific begins hiring Chinese workers.

1865—*April 9:* Confederate General Robert E. Lee surrenders to Union General Ulysses S. Grant, thereby ending the Civil War.

1865—*April 14:* President Abraham Lincoln is shot and killed by John Wilkes Booth.

1865—*Late May:* Supplies and newly discharged soldiers are assembled in Omaha to begin the Union Pacific's full-scale construction efforts.

1865—*Late November:* Civil War hero William T. Sherman inspects the Union Pacific's first fifteen miles of track.

1866—*February 8:* Jack and Dan Casement, two excellent construction bosses, sign on with the Union Pacific.

1866—*Spring:* The Central Pacific begins the painstaking task of drilling tunnels through the Sierras.

1866—*April:* With the help of the Casement invention of the supply train, the Union Pacific begins laying tracks at the rate of one mile a day.

1866—*November:* The Union Pacific chooses North Platte, Nebraska, as its winter quarters; it becomes a Hell on Wheels boom town.

1867—*Spring:* The Central Pacific drags supplies, railroad cars, and locomotives over the Sierras to begin work on the eastern side of the range.

1867—*March:* Anti-Chinese organizations form in California; Chinese workers are brutalized by mobs.

1867—*Summer:* Fighting explodes between the Plains peoples and the Union Pacific crews.

1867—*December:* The Central Pacific completes the Summit Tunnel.

1868—*May:* The Central Pacific's tracks create the new town of Reno, Nevada.

1868—*Summer:* Mormons begin working as graders when the Union Pacific enters Utah.

1868—*December:* At year's end, the Central Pacific has completed 360 miles of track, and the Union Pacific has laid 425 miles.

1869—*April 10:* Congress sets a spot near Ogden, Utah, for the two companies to meet; the spot is later called Promontory Point.

1869—*April 28:* Central Pacific crews lay ten miles of track in one day; the crews capture a record and win a bet for their boss, Charles Crocker.

1869—*May 10:* The Golden Spike ceremony marks the completion of the transcontinental railroad.

★ CHAPTER NOTES ★

Chapter 1
    1. Lynne Rhodes Mayer and Kenneth E. Vose, *Makin' Tracks* (New York: Barnes & Noble Books, 1995), p. 197.
    2. Dee Brown, *Hear That Lonesome Whistle Blow* (New York: Holt, Rinehart and Winston, 1977), p. 133.

Chapter 2
    1. J.S. Holliday, *The World Rushed In: The California Gold Rush Experience, An Eyewitness Account of a Nation Heading West* (New York: Simon and Schuster, 1981), p. 333.
    2. *Annals of America,* vol. 7, p. 87.
    3. Federal Writers Project, *The WPA Guide to California* (New York: Pantheon Books, 1939 and 1984), p. 54.
    4. Dee Brown, *Hear That Lonesome Whistle Blow* (New York: Holt, Rinehart and Winston, 1977), p. 28.
    5. In Holliday, p. 204.
    6. Brown, p. 26.
    7. Robert West Howard, *The Great Iron Trail* (New York: G. P. Putnam's Sons, 1962), p. 98.

Chapter 3
    1. Dee Brown, *Hear That Lonesome Whistle Blow* (New York: Holt, Rinehart and Winston, 1977), p. 8.
    2. *Annals of America,* vol. 9, p. 1.
    3. Lynne Rhodes Mayer and Kenneth E. Vose, *Makin' Tracks* (New York: Barnes & Noble Books, 1995), p. 12.
    4. In Henry Steele Commager, ed., *Documents of American History* (New York: Appleton-Century-Crofts, Inc., 1958), vol. I, pp. 411–412.
    5. Mayer and Vose, p. 19.

Chapter 4
    1. Lynne Rhodes Mayer and Kenneth E. Vose, *Makin' Tracks* (New York: Barnes & Noble Books, 1995), p. 25.
    2. Robert West Howard, *The Great Iron Trail* (New York: G. P. Putnam's Sons, 1962), p. 135.
    3. Mayer and Vose, p. 28.
    4. J.S. Holliday, *The World Rushed In: The California Gold Rush Experience, An Eyewitness Account of a Nation Heading West* (New York: Simon and Schuster, 1981), p. 376.
    5. Mayer and Vose, p. 31.
    6. Howard, p. 34.

Chapter 5
    1. Lynne Rhodes Mayer and Kenneth E. Vose, *Makin' Tracks* (New York: Barnes & Noble Books, 1995), p. 68.
    2. Dee Brown, *Hear That Lonesome Whistle Blow* (New York: Holt, Rinehart and Winston, 1977), p. 54.

3. Ibid., p. 65.

4. In Thomas A. Bailey and David M. Kennedy, eds., *The American Spirit: United States History as Seen by Contemporaries* (Lexington, Mass.: D.C. Heath and Company, 1991), vol. 1, p. 276.

5. Brown, p. 66.

6. Wesley S. Griswold, *A Work of Giants* (New York: McGraw-Hill, 1962), p. 209.

7. Ibid., p. 224.

8. Ibid., p. 223.

Chapter 6

1. Robert West Howard, *The Great Iron Trail* (New York: G. P. Putnam's Sons, 1962), p. 269.

2. Bergen Evans, *Dictionary of Quotations* (New York: Random House, 1969), p. 345.

3. Wesley S. Griswold, *A Work of Giants* (New York: McGraw-Hill, 1962), p. 216.

4. Dee Brown, *Hear That Lonesome Whistle Blow* (New York: Holt, Rinehart and Winston, 1977), p. 74.

5. Griswold, p. 119.

6. In Henry Steele Commager, ed., *Documents of American History* (New York: Appleton-Century-Crofts, Inc., 1958), vol. II, p. 110.

7. Lynne Rhodes Mayer and Kenneth E. Vose, *Makin' Tracks* (New York: Barnes & Noble Books, 1995), p. 106.

Chapter 7

1. Wesley S. Griswold, *A Work of Giants* (New York: McGraw-Hill, 1962), p. 239.

2. Dee Brown, *Hear That Lonesome Whistle Blow* (New York: Holt, Rinehart and Winston, 1977), p. 184.

3. Lynne Rhodes Mayer and Kenneth E. Vose, *Makin' Tracks* (New York: Barnes & Noble Books, 1995), p. 160.

4. Ibid., p. 81.

5. Griswold, p. 310.

6. Ibid., p. 311.

7. Mayer and Vose, p. 164.

8. Ibid., p. 195.

9. Ibid., p. 180.

10. Ibid., p. 198.

11. Brown, pp. 133–135.

Chapter 8

1. Lynne Rhodes Mayer and Kenneth E. Vose, *Makin' Tracks* (New York: Barnes & Noble Books, 1995), p. 193.

2. Dee Brown, *Hear That Lonesome Whistle Blow* (New York: Holt, Rinehart and Winston, 1977), p. 147.

3. Bill Yenne, ed., *All Aboard* (Greenwich, Conn.: Brompton Books, 1989), p. 34.

4. Brown, p. 142.

5. Walt Whitman, "Passage to India," in *The Viking Portable Library, Walt Whitman* (New York: Viking Books, 1965), pp. 343–345.

★ FURTHER READING ★

Fisher, Leonard Everett. *Tracks Across America: The Story of the American Railroad, 1825–1900.* New York: Holiday House, 1992.

Fraser, Mary Ann. *Ten Mile Day and the Building of the Transcontinental Railroad.* New York: Henry Holt, 1993.

Jefferis, David. *Trains: The History of Railroads.* New York: Franklin Watts, 1991.

McNeese, Tim. *America's First Railroads.* New York: Macmillan, 1993.

Miller, Marilyn. *The Transcontinental Railroad.* Parsippany, N.J.: Silver Burdett, 1987.

Scarry, Huck. *Aboard a Steam Locomotive.* New York: Prentice Hall, 1987.

Stein, R. Conrad. *The Story of the Golden Spike.* Danbury, Conn.: Children's Press, 1978.

★ INDEX ★